PILGRIMAGE TO HUMANITY

Albert Schweitzer

PILGRIMAGE TO HUMANITY

Translated by
Walter E. Stuermann
University of Tulsa

A Philosophical Paperback

Philosophical Library
New York

ISBN 8022-2437-7

 The material in this book has been edited by Dr. Rudolf Grabs, and was originally published by Reclam Verlag, Stuttgart, under the title *Weg zur Humanität*. Library of Congress Catalog Card No. 61-15250. Printed in the United States of America.

CONTENTS

PILGRIMAGE TO HUMANITY

The world—majesty masking
the dreadful, the absurd
hidden in the rational,
joy embracing suffering. (1)

EUROPE AND HUMAN CULTURE*

Only an ethical energy can redeem us from our want of culture. (2) What is culture? Its essence is the ethical perfecting of individuals and of society. Every spiritual and material development possesses a meaning for culture. The will to culture is a universal will to progress which recognizes the ethical as the highest value. Apart from all the meaning which we ascribe to the advancement of knowledge and skills, it is clear that only a humanity which strives for ethical ideals can really partake in full

* Schweitzer's "Kultur" is rendered by "culture" rather than, as is commonly the case, by "civilization."

measure of the blessings of material progress. Moreover, only such a humanity can be master among the perils such an advance brings with it. For a generation which exhibits and deems fitting for itself a faith in an immanent, automatic, and naturally realized process of development, ethical ideals are no longer needed. But to live by a faith in the competence of knowledge and skills alone leads to the frightful consequences of error in which we find ourselves. The only possible escape from the present chaos is for us to be guided by a concept of culture in which the ideals of genuine culture are sovereign.

What is the world-view in which the universal will to progress and the ethical will to progress are united and grounded in one another?

It consists in ethical world-affirmation and life-affirmation.

What are world-affirmation and life-affirmation?

For us Europeans and descendants of Europeans, the will to progress is something so natural and self-evident that we no longer recognize that it is rooted in a world-view and springs from a spiritual act. If we look around us in the world, we immediately perceive, however, that what is so obvious to us is really anything but self-evident. (3) The world-view which prevails among a people determines whether or not the will to progress is present. The world-view of world-negation and life-negation precludes it; that of world-affirmation and life-affirmation promotes it. Among primitives and half-primitives, whose undeveloped world-view is not yet related to the problem of world-affirmation or world-negation, no will to progress is present. Their ideal is the simplest and least troublesome sort of life.

As a result of the fortunes of time and because of a transformation in our world-view, we Europeans are enchanted with the will to progress. (4) The struggle for material and spiritual development which prevails among modern European men arises from the world-view which they entertain. In the Renaissance and religious movements connected with it, man became newly related to himself and to the world. This reorientation awakened in him the need to create spiritual and material values which would promote a higher development of men and humanity. Nevertheless, modern European man is not inspired in the direction of progress simply because he hopes personally to profit from it. On the contrary, he is more preoccupied with the fortunes which will befall coming generations than with his own condition. Enthusiasm for progress infuses him. Impressed by the great experiences which the world has evidently produced and preserved for him by the exercise of practical and dynamic powers, he determines that he will himself become a purposeful and vigorous force in the world. With high confidence he looks forward to new and better times which will dawn for mankind; and he understands that the power of the ideals advanced and practiced by the many conquers and transforms the conditions of life. In this will to material progress, which is united with the ethical, modern culture is grounded. (5)

Under the influence of Christianity, philosophical ethics acquired an enthusiasm which was not up to that time characteristic of it. Conversely, as a result of the impact of philosophical energies, Christian ethics began to reflect on what it should really mean and what it must accomplish. From this felicitous fusion, there arose the conviction that ethics could no longer permit what it had earlier allowed, namely, injustices, cruelties, and the heinous effects of superstition. Torture was to be done away with. The scourge of witchcraft trials was to be eliminated. Humane principles were to take the place of inhuman laws. (6) An endeavor to understand the principles and ends of law accompanied the struggle against illegality and inhumane practices. Jeremy Bentham, for example, raised his prophetic voice against laws which permitted usury, foolish customs barriers, and inhuman colonization.

An era of the sovereignty of the practical and the moral appeared on history's horizon. People began to grasp the concepts of duty and honor by which the human community was later nourished. Without alarm, a profound and felicitous reform in conduct was achieved. The education of men for civilized life was carried forward in nobler ways. The public welfare was elevated as a standard of judgment for governments and for their subjects. At the same time, men began to appreciate that every human being should be able to exercise himself in a manner commensurate with his own dignity and welfare. The war against ignorance was under way. (7)

With the discovery that reason teaches the principle of love, there came a reformation which has no equal in the history of humanity. (8)

Nevertheless, the course of modern European thought reveals a tragedy. By a slow but irresistible process, the union of the ethical and world-affirmation and life-affirmation has been dissolving and threatens to disappear completely. Consequently, European humanity is infused and impelled by a will to progress which is superficial and improperly oriented. (9)

In the nineteenth century, the spirit of realism raised its head. . . . The first important personality in which it was incarnate was Napoleon I. The first significant thinker who acted as its prophet was the German philosopher Hegel. According to Hegel, men do not find it necessary to transform reality in order to bring it into conformity with ideals established by thought. Progress itself establishes and preserves the correlation in a natural way. In one way or another, the passions of dominant personalities and of nations subserve progress—even war. The notion that ethical idealism is a kind of sentimentalism, with which one can achieve nothing in the world of reality, originated with Hegel. He voices the theory of realism in a phrase, when he writes, "What is rational is real; and what is real is rational." When this formula was written on June 25, 1820, our age was born—an age which continues to move toward world war and which will perhaps one day destroy culture completely.

Hegel ventures to assert that everything subserves progress. The passions of rulers and nations are servants of progress. We can only say that Hegel did not know national passions as we know them; otherwise he would not have dared to write that! . . . Will we be able again to entertain and exercise ideals which can transform reality? This is the question before us today. (10)

A proper understanding of the laws and limits of human thought is required if we are to clear the building site for the construction of a future philosophy. . . . As great and as significant as the progress of natural science has been, the materialistic philosophy bound up with it will be of no help. It will always display the same poverty and the same radical errors. Although some distinguished scientific scholars have recognized this, materialism nevertheless continues to believe that its future is firmly fixed by the development of natural science. . . . For the foreseeable future, materialism will remain the philosophical religion of truncated intellects. Consequently, Feuerbach is destined to be resurrected in many editions and in many periodicals. (11)

Our philosophy incorporates only unstable fragments of an edifying world-view which hovers before it. As a result, our culture remains fragmentary and insecure.

It was disastrous that western thinkers did not confess the unsatisfactory results and the futility of their search for a secure, valuable world-view. Our philosophy became more and more superficial. Thinkers lost touch with the elemental questions which man has posed about life and the world. More and more they found themselves gorged on a diet of pedantic philosophical questions and of the professional manipulation of philosophical technicalities. Instead of producing genuine philosophy, they concocted in a professional and perfunctory manner an impotent brew. Often their maneuvers were versatile and professional, but the results were nevertheless impotence and irrelevance.

This artificial philosophizing failed to grapple with a world-view founded in thought and directed to the service of life. Through it we lost an invigorating world-view and, consequently, culture.

Some signs of self-reflection are beginning, however, to make their appearance. Here and there we discover a recognition that a philosophy must again be sought which will offer men a meaningful world-view. (12)

The mind of mankind must be renewed, if it is not to go down to destruction. (13)

When the thought of future thinkers moves to a

deeper, more ethical will to progress, we will be redeemed from our want of culture and its attendant miseries and move toward genuine culture. Sooner or later that true and definitive renaissance which brings peace to the world must dawn. (14)

AFRICAN PROBLEMS

When I am in a boat with Africans who ask what is different in Europe from what it is here, I describe three of the most striking things. At one time or another, most of the Africans connected with the Lambaréné hospital have heard me speak of them. Repetition brings them as new to their ears. They continue to be amazed by them and to comment on them.

First, I tell them that there are forest fires in Europe. This they cannot understand, for even in the dry season here it is so damp that the forest cannot catch fire, no matter what one does to set it ablaze. Even trees which are cut in the dry season and left to dry for months cannot easily be burned. Only the small and middle-sized branches are consumed. The large branches and the great trunks are simply charred.

At the sawmills here, owner and workers smoke their pipes and shake out the glowing embers into the sawdust. It is so damp that there is no danger of fire. The African cannot understand that in Europe a forest fire may be started by someone dropping a burning match.

After they have made their comments on this remarkable event, I tell them that in Europe people row boats for pleasure. This revelation is greeted with unrestrained laughter and a flood of questions. "Who orders them to row?" "No one." "Someone must give them a gift for doing it." "No, they do it willingly and for nothing. They often row until they are completely exhausted!"

Their remarks on this matter are apparently endless. Here in Africa, if the men in two canoes are going upstream or downstream together, they may race each other for a short distance. But the idea that people will get into a boat, not wanting to go on a journey or without articles to be transported, simply in order to row is incomprehensible for the African. Furthermore, the idea that they will use their leisure time in this senseless activity is incredible. I do not attempt to make clear to them what sport is. Their life is such that they have to use their physical energies more than they like. Consequently, they cannot understand how people will exert themselves when not forced to do so.

The third thing I tell them is that in Europe a man can marry without having to pay for his wife.

This cannot be true, they say. The doctor is having some fun at the expense of the poor black man. (15)

Among primitive people, taboo is extremely important. Taboo means that something must be avoided, lest misfortune or death results. The origin of taboo ideas is a dark matter. Some taboos have significance for all members of a group. Others have a meaning only for certain individuals. Among those of general significance, there are the important taboos to be observed by a man whose wife is expecting a child. The Pahouin taboo forbids him to eat meat which has begun to smell (apart from the taboo, the natives readily eat meat which is almost putrid), to touch a chameleon, to fill a hole with earth, to drive nails, to be present at the death of a man or a beast, to have anything to do with a dead body, to step over a procession of driver ants, and to do many other things.

At one time I was upset when Africans absolutely refused to carry the bier at hospital funerals. By presents and pressure, I tried to persuade them, when their turn came. A man would fall on his knees, begging me to release him from the task. Since then I have come to appreciate the inner conflicts my requests produced. Nowadays I use only volunteers for this duty, and they receive a fixed wage for their service. (16)

There is nothing in the life of these people which cannot become the object of a taboo. (17) Some women have the idea that, if their first child is a boy, either they or the child must die. . . . The fact that some Africans die if their taboo is violated can only be explained on the ground that their belief in taboo affects them mentally in a way beyond our ability to imagine. Certain Europeans who have earned the confidence of the Africans can accomplish something in such cases by their spiritual authority. (18) For the African, Christianity is the light which shines in the darkness of fear. It assures him that he is not under the control of nature-spirits, ancestral gods, or fetishes. It testifies that no man exercises any uncanny power over another. It signifies that only God's will is sovereign in all events.

"I lay in cruel bondage,
Thou cam'st and mad'st me free!"

The words of Paul Gerhardt's advent hymn express better than any others what Christianity means for primitive man. (19)

Speaking of my work in the primeval forest of Equatorial Africa provides an opportunity to express myself on the difficult problems of colonization among primitive people.

Do we Europeans have the right to impose our rule on primitive and half-primitive people? No, if we desire only to rule and to get material gain from their lands. Yes, if we seriously intend to educate them and to help them realize a condition of well-being. Were it really possible for them to live unto themselves, we could leave them to their own devices. But the fact is that international trade has made its impact on them. Neither we nor they can undo this. Already they have lost their freedom because of it. Their economic and social fabric has been transformed by it. As a result, the chiefs, by use of the weapons and wealth international trade has brought to them, reduce the mass of the natives to servitude and turn them into slaves who are required to work for the export trade in order to enrich the few. Moreover, sometimes people themselves become merchandise to be exchanged for money, lead, gunpowder, tobacco, and liquor, just as in the days of slave trading. In face of the situation produced by the advent of international trade, there is no question of real freedom of self-determination. It is only a question as to whether native peoples are to be left to the mercies, good and evil, of greedy native rulers or to be ruled by officials of European nations.

Many of those who undertook, in our name, to seize colonial lands were guilty of acts of injustice, violence, and cruelty which were just as offensive as those of the native rulers. A heavy load of guilt, therefore, rests upon us. Not one of the sins committed against native peoples today should be buried in silence or excused. (20)

The tragic fact is that the interests of colonization and those of civilization are not commensurate. On the contrary, they are in many ways at war with each other. It would be best for primitive peoples to be left, while isolated as much as possible from international trade, to work out slowly under perceptive guidance their development from a nomadic or half-nomadic state to the point where they became settled agriculturalists and artisans. This is, however, impossible because they will not restrain themselves before the invitation to earn money by selling to the markets of international trade, and international trade will not refuse to purchase goods from them by exchanging manufactured items. It is therefore extremely difficult to carry forward a colonization which at the same time promotes true civilization. Real wealth for native peoples would be found in their producing, as far as possible, the necessities of life by their own agricultural and handicraft efforts. Unfortunately they think only of producing what international trade will use and that for which it will pay well. With the money they receive, they buy manufactured items and processed foods. Native industry is thus made impossible, and frequently their own agricultural pursuits are jeopardized. This is the unfortunate situation of the primitive and half-primitive peoples who can offer international trade rice, cotton, coffee, cocoa, minerals, timber, and other goods. (21)

The problems of native education are entangled with those of economics and social affairs and they are just as complicated as the latter. Agriculture and crafts are the foundation of culture. Only where they are present do we have the necessary ground for the formation and continued existence of a level of population which can pursue commercial and intellectual interests. But in dealing with the natives among the colonies, we begin—and they demand it themselves—as if reading and writing were the beginnings of culture, not agriculture and crafts. In schools which are organized on the European model, we produce "educated persons," who think themselves above manual labor and want to engage only in commercial and intellectual pursuits. When they are not able to find suitable employment in business or government offices, they sit around as idlers and grumblers. (22)

In a particularly difficult period in our African work, Minköe, a promising helper, left me. He acted as foreman for construction work and for the care of the patients' quarters. He had discovered that this sort of work was beneath him. People had also told him that so talented a young man should not waste away in the role of a handy man and orderly for the doctor. So he determined to attend the "high school" which would open its doors at the nearby Mission Station in November. In order to be adequately prepared for the studies facing him, he must meanwhile give his brain some rest. Thus he left me immediately, while our hands were full of things to do, if we were to complete the necessary work before the advent of the rainy season. While he played the role of intellectual, I had to trouble myself with the business of lumber and bamboo and take his place wielding hammer and saw. . . .

In the middle of September, the first rains fall. The cry then goes up to get all the building timber under cover. Since we have scarcely an able-bodied man in the hospital, I begin, with the help of two faithful workers, to drag the beams and boards. Then I see an African in white clothing sitting by a patient he has come to visit. "Say friend," I call, "won't you give us a little help?" "I am an intellectual—I don't drag timber," comes the answer. "You're lucky," I respond. "I wanted to be an intellectual too, but I didn't make it." (23)

In almost all the colonies, the battle against disease has been launched too late and with too little vigor. We may thank modern medical science and its techniques that it can be carried forward today with some hope of success. It is often contended that we should bring medical aid to the colonies because, without it, the colonies would become worthless. We have here, however, something more important than an economic issue. It is inconceivable that civilized peoples should keep to themselves the means modern science provides for fighting diseases, pain, and death. If there is any ethical sensitivity among us, we cannot do anything else but use the new tools of medicine to serve those in distant lands who are in greater physical distress than we. In addition to the physicians who are sent out by European governments and who can accomplish only a part of what is required, others must go also, commissioned by the human community as such. Those of us who through our experience have come to know what pain and anxiety are must endeavor to extend to others in physical distress the sort of help we have received. We are no longer our own—we are brothers to all who suffer. . . .

By faith in the fundamental truth which is expressed in the concept of the "Fellowship of Those Who Bear the Mark of Pain," I established the hospital at Lambaréné. Above all, it affirms that whatever good we do for colonial peoples is not charity but atonement for the great suffering we have brought them from the first days that our ships found their ways to their lands. As we face them today, colonial problems cannot be solved by political measures alone. European and African must encounter one another in a new ethical spirit. Only then will understanding be possible.

Let us strive to create this spirit. It will make world politics a fountain of blessings for the future. (24)

THE STORY OF MY LIFE

DEVELOPMENT

I was born on January 14, 1875, at Kaysersberg in Upper Alsace, the second child of pastor Ludwig Schweitzer, who served a small evangelical congregation there. My grandfather on my father's side was a school teacher and organist at Pfaffenhofen in Lower Alsace. Three of his brothers were of similar calling. My mother, Adele, whose maiden name was Schillinger, was the daughter of the pastor of Mühlbach in the Münster Valley (Upper Alsace).

A few weeks after my birth, my father came to Günsbach in the Münster Valley. There I lived a very happy childhood with my three sisters and a brother, troubled only by my father's frequent illnesses. Later his health improved. Indeed, while a robust seventy years of age, he ministered to his parish during the war, under the fire of the French guns which looked down on the Valley from the Vosges mountains and which took their toll of the houses and inhabitants of Günsbach. He died at an advanced age in 1925. My mother was run down by cavalry and killed on the road between Günsbach and Weier-im-Tal in 1916.

When I was five years old, my father began to instruct me on grandfather Schillinger's old piano. While he had no great technical ability, he improvised beautifully. When I was seven I surprised my school teacher by playing on the harmonium some hymns for which I supplied my own harmonies. At eight I began to play the organ, although my legs were scarcely long enough to reach the pedals. I derived my love for the organ from my grandfather Schillinger, who had busied himself with organs and organ-playing. My mother told me that he was noted for improvising excellently. . . . I first took the place of the organist for the service at Günsbach when I was nine years old.

I attended the village school at Günsbach until the autumn of 1884. After that I was in the *Realschule* . . . at Münster for a year. During this time I took private lessons in Latin in order to prepare for the Fifth Form of the Gymnasium. In the autumn of 1885, I entered the Gymnasium at Mülhausen in Alsace. (25)

When I look back upon my youth, I am moved by the thought of all the people I have to thank for what they gave to me or meant to me. Yet I am plagued by the consciousness that, while I was young, I did not really show them proper gratitude. How many have departed this life without my having expressed to them what it meant for me to receive kindness and care from them. Often I have shamefully and quietly uttered words of gratitude over the graves of those to whom I should have spoken while they were still living.

For this reason I believe I can say that I was not ungrateful. I early awakened from that youthful thoughtlessness which reckoned the goodness and care I received from people as something self-evident. (26)

On June 18, 1893, I passed the final examination. (27) At the end of October, I enrolled in the University of Strasbourg. It was then in its prime. Chained by no traditions, teachers and students strove to realize the ideal of a modern university.... I attended lectures in the faculties of theology and philosophy. (28)

In the year following April 1, 1894, I discharged my responsibilities for military service. (29)

The years of study at Strasbourg passed quickly. At the end of the summer of 1897 I stood for the first theological examination. (30)

On the advice of Theobald Ziegler, I next undertook the dissertation for the degree of doctor of philosophy. At the end of the semester, in a chat under an umbrella on the University steps, he indicated that my research should be in the religious philosophy of Immanuel Kant. This pleased me very much. Near the end of October, 1898, I traveled to Paris in order to study philosophy at the Sorbonne and to continue organ studies under Widor. (31)

The doctoral research did not suffer damage either from my devotion to art or from my social obligations, because my health permitted extensive studies at night. Sometimes I played for Widor in the morning without having been to bed. (32)

In the middle of March, 1899, I returned to Strasbourg and presented my finished work to Theobald Ziegler. He expressed strong agreement with it. My degree would be awarded at the end of July.

In the summer of 1899, I was in Berlin and invested my time chiefly in philosophical studies. My desire was to read the major works of ancient and modern philosophy. I also heard the lectures of Harnack, Pfleiderer, Kaftan, Paulsen, and Simmel. While at first I only occasionally went to Simmel's lectures, later I became a regular attendant. . . . In Berlin, I spent much time with Karl Stumpf. His psychological studies of feeling for tone were of great interest to me. . . . With the exception of Egidi, the Berlin organists were somewhat disappointing. They tried more for outward virtuosity than for true plasticity of style, which Widor emphasized heavily. And how dull and dry was the sound of the new Berlin organs in comparison with the instruments of Cavaillé-Coll in St. Sulpice and Notre Dame.

Professor Heinrich Reimann, organist at the Kaiser

Wilhelm Memorial Church, to whom I brought a letter of introduction from Widor, hired me as his substitute when he was away. Through him I came to know some Berlin musicians, painters, and sculptors.

At the home of the widow of Ernst Curtius, a well-known Hellenist, I got to know the academic world. She kindly introduced me as a friend of her stepson. . . . Even today I reckon it a striking piece of good fortune to have been able in her home to get to know the leaders of Berlin's intellectual life at that time.

Berlin's intellectual life impressed me more than that of Paris. In the latter—world-city though it was—the intellectual life was fragmented. A person had to be completely accustomed to it before he could make a judgment about the values existing in it. On the other hand, in Berlin the intellectual life was centered in its highly organized university, which was itself a living organism. (33)

At the end of July, 1899, I returned to Strasbourg and received my doctor's degree. Ziegler and Windelband agreed that in my oral examination I did not perform as well as they expected from my dissertation. The dissertation appeared in 1899 as a book with the title *The Religious Philosophy of Kant from the "Critique of Pure Reason" to "Religion within the Bounds of Reason Alone."*

Theobald Ziegler suggested that I undertake the duties of *Privat-dozent* in philosophy. I decided, however, for the theological assignment and remained in Strasbourg from then on. The task of correcting the proofs of my doctor's dissertation was scarcely complete when I set to work to achieve the theological Licentiate. (34)

On December 1, 1899, I secured an appointment as preacher at the Church of St. Nicholas in Strasbourg. First I was a so-called *"Lehrvikar."* When I passed my second theological examination, I became a curate.

This second theological examination, which was conducted by elderly clergymen, I passed on July 15, 1900, only with great difficulty. Since I was preoccupied with the dissertation for the Licentiate, I had neglected to refresh my knowledge of the different departments of theology on which this examination was given. (35)

My afternoon sermons, which I conceived as devotionals rather than as sermons, were so short that at one time certain groups in the congregation complained to Mr. Knittel, who held the post of "Inspector in Spiritual Matters." He had to summon me before him on this issue, but he was as embarrassed about it as I was. When he wanted to know what he was to say to those who felt themselves aggrieved, I responded that he should tell them that I was only a poor curate who stopped talking when he discovered he had nothing else to say about the text. (36)

Three times a week after classes, I conducted from eleven to twelve o'clock the confirmation classes for boys. I tried to give them the least possible outside work so that the sessions we had together would be periods of untroubled renewal of spirit and heart. The last ten minutes of the sessions I devoted to having them repeat after me and commit to memory biblical texts and verses of hymns which they could take with them through life for guidance. I conceived the goal of my instruction to be that of inserting in their hearts and minds the truths of the Gospel and of making them religious in such a way that later they would resist the temptations of irreligion. I also sought to awaken in them a love for the church and a sense of need for the Sunday hour of meditation. I taught them respect for the traditional doctrines, but at the same time to hold to Paul's principle that where the spirit of Christ is present, there is freedom. . . . In the course of these religious studies, I became aware of how much of a residue of the school teacher was left in me from my ancestors. (37)

One distinct advantage of my position was that it left me adequate time for scientific work and music. . . . In this simple way the stream of my life flowed during the years which were so critical for my creative work. I worked at length and with unbroken concentration but without haste.

Since I had neither time nor money, I did not travel much. . . . When my savings allowed, I made the pilgrimage to Bayreuth when it was a festival year. (38)

On July 21, 1900, my work on the problem of the Last Supper earned for me the degree of Licentiate in Theology. A second work, *The Secret of the Messiahship and the Passion,* secured for me in 1902 the position of *Privat-dozent* at the University. (39)

On March 1, 1902, I delivered my inaugural address before the Strasbourg theological faculty. It was on the Logos doctrine in the Gospel of John. (40) My lectures began in the summer semester of 1902 with a course on the Pastoral Epistles.

It was some conversations with students which moved me to my study of the history of research on the life of Jesus. They reported that they had not learned anything about previous research on this topic in their studies. . . . (41) My *Quest of the Historical Jesus* appeared as early as 1906. (42) While I was involved in this research, I completed in French my book on J. S. Bach. . . . During 1903 and 1904, I invested all my free time in the study of this musician. (43)

It was, indeed, a bold undertaking for me to write a book on Bach! While I had read some in the history and theory of music, my studies were not those of a professional. I had no intention of turning up new material on Bach and his times. As a musician, I simply wanted to talk to musicians about Bach. I intended briefly to treat what had been handled too cursorily in previous works, namely, the essential meaning of Bach's music and the proper way of rendering it. Consequently, the biographical material in the book is merely introductory. (44)

It delighted me that the book met with recognition in Germany as an introduction to Bach research. . . . In *Kunstwart,* von Lüpke asked about a translation. But when I undertook the job, I was soon convinced that I would not be capable of satisfactorily translating myself. . . . So, I put the French Bach aside and determined to produce a new and better German one. The publisher was amazed to discover that the 455-page book grew into one of 844 pages. (45)

The German edition appeared at the beginning of 1908. From it the English translation was made. . . . (46)

In connection with the work on Bach, I published in the autumn of 1905, before my medical studies began, an essay on organ building.

It was from my grandfather Schillinger that I derived the interest in organ building, which, even when I was a boy, moved me to learn all about the insides of organs. (47)

Slowly attention was drawn to the idea of a reform of organ-building which I advanced in my essay. At the Congress of the International Music Society at Vienna in 1909 . . . there appeared for the first time a section on organ building. Some colleagues and I worked out "International Regulations for Organ Building," which attempted to wipe out the blind admiration for purely technical improvements and called for carefully built organs of beautiful tone. As years passed, I began to understand more and more that the good organ must unite the tone qualities of the old instrument with the technical advances in the new one. Twenty-two years after its appearance, my essay on organ building was able to be republished, without change, as containing the acceptable principles of reform in this field. With the addition of an appendix on the present state of the organ building industry, it appeared as a jubilee edition. (48)

I have given much time and energy to the struggle for the true organ. Many a night I have spent over organ plans which had to be approved or revised. And I have undertaken many a journey in order to study the question of restoring or rebuilding an organ. . . . How often were these many letters, journeys, and conversations in vain, because the people involved decided for the factory organ, whose plans looked so fine on paper!

The hardest fights were those in behalf of preserving old organs. . . . The first old organ which I saved—with much trouble—was the excellent work of Silberman at St. Thomas' in Strasbourg.

My friends used to say, "In the South he rescues old Africans, in the North old organs." (49)

On Friday, October 13, 1905, I dropped some letters into a mailbox on the Avenue de la Grande Armée in Paris. They were addressed to my parents and to my friends. In them I said that I was going to become a medical student at the beginning of the winter semester and that I would later go as a doctor to Equatorial Africa. . . . The plan I now set in motion had been with me for a long time. Its origin was to be found in my student days. It was incomprehensible to me that I should lead a happy life when so many people around me were struggling with suffering and grief. . . . On a bright summer morning in the Whitsuntide holiday in 1896 at Günsbach, I awoke with the thought that my good fortune was not to be taken as something self-evident. . . . In peaceful reflection, while the birds were singing, I decided before I got up that I would be justified in devoting myself until I was thirty to science and art in order to give myself thereafter to direct services to humanity. . . . It was not yet clear to me what the exact nature of the activities I thus planned would be. I left it to circumstances to determine them. But one thing was certain. However insignificant it might appear, the goal must be a direct service of humanity. (50)

One morning in the autumn of 1904 I found on my writing table one of the green-covered magazines in which the Paris Missionary Society reported each month its activities. . . . My eye fell on an article with the title "The Needs of the Congo Mission." When I finished reading the article, I serenely began my work. My search was over. (51)

Several months later, I spent my thirtieth birthday like the man in the parable who wants to build a tower and estimates whether he has the resources to complete the job. I finally decided to realize my plan for service to humanity through work in Equatorial Africa. (52)

What seemed most senseless to my friends was that I wanted to go to Africa as a physician, not a missionary. This meant at thirty years of age a long, difficult period of training. I had no doubt myself that the project would require an exceptional effort. . . . I wanted to be a doctor so I could serve without having to talk. . . . My calling as theological teacher and preacher was certainly a source of satisfaction to me. This new calling appeared to me, however, to be a matter of putting the religion of love to work rather than of talking about it. (53)

At the beginning of my medical course, I was hard pressed by financial problems. Later my situation improved because of the success of my German Bach and because of concert fees I earned. In October, 1911, I took the state medical examination. . . . On December 17, I took my last examination under Madelung, the surgeon. When I left the hospital to step into the cold darkness outside, I had difficulty appreciating that the tremendous effort of medical training was now behind me. Over and over, I had to assure myself that I was not dreaming but awake. As we walked along, Madelung's voice seemed to fall in from a great distance: "Only because of your good health were you able to finish that task." (54)

Even while I was busy with my medical studies, I was making preparations for the journey to Africa. Early in 1912, I resigned from my teaching duties at the University and from my post at St. Nicholas'. . . . To give up preaching and teaching represented a very great personal loss. . . . Finally I also gave up my residence on St. Thomas Embankment in order that with my wife—Helen Bresslau, daughter of the Strasbourg historian, whom I married on June 18, 1912—I might spend my last months in my father's parsonage at Günsbach. . . .

I spent the spring of 1912 in Paris studying tropical medicine and purchasing things for Africa. (55)

When I was sure I could summon the means for founding a small hospital, I made a definite offer to the Paris Missionary Society to come and serve at my own expense as a mission doctor at Lambaréné in its mission field on the River Ogowé. . . . About a year later, I had secured the funds necessary for the trip to Lambaréné and for the operation of the hospital during its first year. Some wealthy friends permitted me to think that they would again give help when my funds were exhausted. (56)

In February, 1913, the seventy crates were prepared and sent as freight to Bordeaux. (57) On the afternoon of Good Friday, 1913, my wife and I left Günsbach. In the evening of March 26, we embarked at Bordeaux. (58)

LAMBARÉNÉ

At Lambaréné the missionaries cordially received us. Unfortunately they had not been able to construct the small buildings of corrugated sheet-iron in which I was to begin my medical work. The necessary workers had not been hired. . . . At first I had to make use of an old chicken house which stood next to our residence. In late autumn I was able to move into a corrugated-iron building with a palm-leaf roof down by the river. Only eight meters long and four meters wide, it contained a small consulting room and an even smaller dispensary. Eventually there appeared around this unit a string of large bamboo huts for the native patients. The European patients were put up in the mission establishment and in the doctor's house.

From the first days, before I even had time to unpack the medicines and instruments, I was beset by patients. (58) The choice of Lambaréné as the site for the hospital proved to be wise. Native patients could be brought to me by canoe on the River Ogowé from distances of two hundred or three hundred kilometers upstream and downstream. The chief diseases I had to cope with were malaria, leprosy, sleeping sickness, dysentery, frambesia, and phagedenic ulcers. I was startled by the number of cases of pneumonia and heart disease which came to me. There were also many urinary diseases to be treated. Surgery was demanded chiefly by hernia and elephantiasis tumors. Among the natives of Equatorial Africa, hernias are much more common than among Europeans. In the absence of medical treatment, many suffer painful deaths each year due to strangulated hernia, from which they could have been saved by timely surgery. My first surgical case was of this kind.

During my first weeks it became clear that physical suffering was even greater among the Africans than I had supposed. How glad I was that, in spite of all objections, I had persevered in my plan to serve here as a doctor! . . .

At the beginning of my service, I was greatly troubled because I could not find natives to serve as interpreters and orderlies. The first one who proved to be of any help had formerly been a cook. . . . He remained with me in spite of the fact that I could not pay him as much as he received in his former work. Moreover, he gave me some very good advice about dealing with Africans. On one point, which seemed most important to him, I could not follow through. He told me to refuse to treat the persons whose lives I was not likely to save. Repeatedly he pointed to the example of the fetish doctors, who turned aside such cases so that their reputations would not be jeopardized. . . .

Since my wife had been trained as a nurse, she was able to render service in the hospital. She did so courageously, caring for the dangerously ill. In addition, she handled the supply of linen and bandages and took care of the instruments in the dispensary. She made the preparations for the operations and administered the anesthetics. . . . It was a tremendous achievement for her to spend these hours in the hospital, while managing the complicated affairs of an African household.

Within a few months the hospital was providing daily accommodations for forty patients. Beyond this, it was also necessary to furnish lodging for their companions who brought them to the hospital and would stay in order to take them back home.

While the work itself was hard enough, it did not weigh upon me as heavily as the care and responsibilities it entailed. . . .

Insofar as it was possible, I required that my African patients express their gratitude for the help they received in some concrete fashion. Repeatedly I reminded them that the benefits they received from the hospital were the result of sacrifices by many Europeans and that they, in turn, must help keep it going. Eventually I was able to establish the custom of having them pay for the medicines with money, bananas, poultry, or eggs. Of course, what I received was much less in value than the actual cost of the services and medicines. It was, however, a measure of help in supporting the work of the hospital. With the bananas I could feed the patients whose supplies were exhausted. If the bananas gave out, I could buy rice with the money. . . . Of course, I did not demand gifts from the very poor and the very old—and among primitive peoples to be old is to be poor.

The real savages had quite a different interpretation of a gift. When they left the hospital cured, they asked one from me, because now I was their friend. (59)

Preaching brought me considerable pleasure. It was a splendid experience to be able to present the messages of Jesus and Paul to persons to whom they were entirely new. The native teachers from the Mission School acted as translators, rendering each of my sentences immediately into the language of the Galoas or the Pahouins or both.

The small amount of free time I had during my first year at Lambaréné was invested in the last three volumes of the American edition of Bach's organ music.

For my organ playing, I had the splendid piano with pedal attachment, built especially for the tropics, which the Paris Bach Society had given to me as a gift for my years of service as their organist. At first I was not in the mood to practice, for I had envisaged my African service as meaning the end of my career as an artist. Thus, I thought it would be easier to reconcile myself to this situation if I allowed my fingers and feet to lose their dexterity. But one evening as I was playing a Bach organ fugue, in a melancholy mood, the thought struck me that I could use my free hours in Africa for improving and deepening my technique. Immediately I conceived the plan of taking up in succession and learning in detail and by heart compositions by Bach, Mendelssohn, Widor, César Franck, and Max Reger, even if I had to spend weeks or months on a given piece. (60)

My wife and I had now spent our second dry season in Africa. We were beginning to plan a return home at the beginning of the third when we heard, on August 5, 1914, that war had broken out in Europe. (61)

Fortunately, my medicines and dressings did not run out. On the last ship to arrive before the outbreak of war I had received a great supply of materials. (62)

Our health is not excellent, but it is not really bad. Tropical anemia has, of course, set in. It exhibits itself in intense fatigue. Although the walk from the hospital to my residence is but four minutes, it exhausts me. And we sense in ourselves another of its symptoms, namely, great nervousness. . . .

In spite of the anemia and fatigue, I have been able to preserve my mental alertness. If the day has not been too much of a physical strain, I can spend two hours after supper on my work on ethics and culture in the history of human thought. . . . My desk stands before the lattice door which leads out on the veranda. Here I am able to get as much of the evening breeze as possible. The palms rustle lightly as the crickets and toads join in loud music. Harsh and strange cries issue from the forest. My faithful dog, Caramba, growls gently to make his presence known. A small dwarf antelope lies at my feet under the desk. In this solitude, I summon the thoughts which have been within me since 1900, in order to give some help in the restoration of culture. Solitude of the primeval forest!—how can I ever express my gratitude for what you have meant to me? (63)

We spent the rainy season of 1916-17 on the coast because my wife's health had suffered from the sultry air at Lambaréné. A timber merchant permitted us to use a house at Chienga near Cape Lopez at the mouth of one of the branches of River Ogowé. It had been the home of an employee. Because of the war, it was empty. As an expression of my gratitude, I joined his African workmen in rolling okoume logs to shore so that, in the long period they might have to wait before being shipped to Europe, they might not fall victims to the bore-worm. Often it took hours to roll one of these two- or three-ton logs onto the shore. The work had to be done, therefore, at high tide. While the tide was out, I worked on my manuscript on philosophy of culture, if my time was not required by patients. (64)

In September, 1917 . . . the order came that we were immediately to be taken by ship to Europe and placed in a prisoner-of-war camp. Fortunately, the ship was several days late. With the aid of the missionaries and some Africans, we therefore had time to pack our medicines, instruments, and belongings in cases for storage in a small building of corrugated iron....

Two days before our departure I had to operate on a strangulated hernia in the midst of packed and half-packed cases.

As we were being taken aboard the river steamer and while the natives were calling out farewell from the shore, the father superior of the Catholic mission came aboard. With an authoritative gesture, he waved aside the African soldiers who moved to prevent his coming to us. "You shall not leave this land without my thanking you both for all the good that you have done for it," he said. We were never to see him again. Shortly after the war he went down in the Bay of Biscay with the *Afrique,* the very ship which took us to Europe. (65)

When in the middle of July, 1920, I left Swedish soil, where I had been so generously treated, I resolved again to take up my work at Lambaréné. Up to this time I had not dared to think of it. (66)

On February 4, 1924, I departed from Strasbourg. This time my wife could not come with me because of her health. . . . At the hospital site there stood only a small corrugated-iron building and the hardwood frame of one of the big bamboo huts. During the seven years I was away, all the other buildings had decayed or been broken down. . . . First we had to repair the rotten and leaky roofs of the doctor's residence and the two hospital buildings which still stood. I next rebuilt the fallen hospital buildings. This work took many months. It was so exhausting that I could not, as I had planned, give my evenings to revisions of the manuscript, *The Mysticism of St. Paul,* which was begun in 1911 and which I had now brought a second time to Africa.

The round of my life was physician in the mornings and master builder in the afternoons. Just as in my first venture here, no workers were available. All the labor was consumed by the flourishing timber trade, which revived after the war.

I had to make do with a few "volunteers" who came to the hospital as companions for the patients or were convalescents. They worked with no enthusiasm and, if it suited them, they found it convenient to disappear on their work days. . . .

The number of patients kept increasing. As a result, in 1924 and 1925 I sent to Europe for two doctors and two nurses.

In the autumn of 1925, the hospital was for the most part rebuilt. . . . Then a severe famine set in, because throughout the territory the cultivation of foods had been neglected for the cutting of timber. At the same time, we were afflicted by a terrible epidemic of dysentery. These two events kept my helpers and I busy for many months. We had to make numerous trips in our two motorboats, *Tack sa mycket* and *Raarup* (one a gift from Swedish friends, the other from Jutland friends), in order to secure rice wherever possible, if nothing else was available for our hospital's inmates. (67)

The dysentery epidemic proved to me that it was necessary to move the hospital to a larger site. It could not be placed on the mission property, because all the land at my disposal there was shut in by water, swamp, or steep hills. The buildings which could be placed on it would be adequate for the fifty patients and their attendants for whom we had earlier provided, but not for the hundred and fifty who now required our care. . . . The dysentery epidemic also demonstrated something else—the danger to the hospital because of its lacking an isolation ward for infectious cases. Since I could not separate dysentery patients from the others, the whole hospital was being infected. It was a frightful time!

The lack of room for the mentally ill was another serious disadvantage. . . .

With great reluctance, then, I forced myself to move the hospital to a site three kilometers up the river where it could be expanded at will. Trusting in the support of friends of my work, I replaced the old bamboo huts, whose roofs were always needing repairs, with corrugated-iron structures on piles. . . .

As soon as the building site was cleared, I began to prepare the surrounding land for cultivation. What a joy it was to win fields from the forest!

Year after year since then, we have struggled to

produce a Garden of Eden around the hospital. Already we have hundreds of young fruit trees growing. . . . (68)

The fact that I had earlier rebuilt the old hospital rather than immediately building a new one was no real setback. We had acquired many experiences which were now invaluable to us. (69)

On January 21, 1927, when some of the buildings were complete, we transferred the patients to the new hospital. On the last trip that evening, I brought the mentally ill to the new site. Their caretakers never stopped telling them that in the new hospital they would be housed in cells with wooden floors. The old ones had floors of damp earth. . . . For the first time since I began work in Africa, my patients were provided for in a humane fashion! . . .

By the middle of the summer, I completed several more wards. Now I had a hospital in which, if necessary, I could provide for two hundred patients and their companions. (70)

On my third arrival at Lambaréné (at the end of 1929), I found other building projects awaiting me. During a dysentery epidemic, which was coming to an end as I arrived, the wards had been found inadequate. . . . The cells for the mentally ill had to be taken by the dysentery cases. Now quarters for the former had to be constructed. The new cells were made stronger. They were also constructed so as to allow more sunlight and more air to come in. After that I had to build a large ward with individual beds for the very ill, an airy and secure room for food supplies, and rooms for the African orderlies. With the help of our African carpenter, Monenzali, I completed these projects in a year's time, while continuing, of course, my work in the hospital. . . .

Around Easter, 1930, my wife returned to Europe because the climate was making inroads on her health. . . .

Nowadays the hospital is known throughout an area hundreds of kilometers from the site. Some patients spend weeks traveling to the hospital for operations. Through the kindness of friends in Europe, the hospital has an operating room with all the necessary equipment. They have also seen to it that our dispensary contains an adequate store of medicines and drugs, including the special ones required for treating colonial diseases. Furthermore, we are able to feed the many patients who are too poor to buy their own food. So, now it is fine to be at work in Lambaréné, especially since we now have enough doctors and nurses to carry forward the work without having to work to exhaustion. How can we adequately thank the friends of the hospital for making this work possible?

Since the hospital work, while difficult, is no longer "beyond our power," I am fresh enough in the evenings to devote myself to intellectual endeavors. Of course, this must be interrupted, sometimes for days and weeks, when I am so full of anxiety over surgical cases and serious medical cases that I cannot think of anything else. (71)

Satisfactions have come my way. I am called to the service of mercy. My work has been successful. I received much love and kindness from others. I have faithful helpers who make my duties theirs. My health permits the most strenuous kind of work. I possess a temperament which gives me stability and an energy which expresses itself with calmness and deliberation. Finally, whatever good fortune befalls me, I can recognize it as such and receive it as something for which I must bring an offering of thanksgiving.

I am deeply moved by the fact that I am a free man in a time when oppressive lack of freedom is the misfortune of so many. Moreover, I am deeply grateful for the fact that, though my immediate work is material, I have the opportunity to invest myself in the sphere of intellectual activities. (72)

IN THE SECOND WORLD WAR

On January 12, 1939, I left Lambaréné after a two-year stay in order to travel to Europe, where I intended to spend a few months. From the beginning, it was impossible to feel any real joy about the period of relaxation before me. The reports of the course of political events in Europe called forth too great an anxiety and sorrow. In all the ports in which we stopped, we saw warships which symbolized the menace of war. What reports or rumors came over the loudspeakers on the deck and in the dining room or were passed on in conversation were not such as to dispel apprehension—they simply reinforced it.

Upon landing at Bordeaux, I decided to forego the European sojourn and in twelve days to return to Africa by the same ship on which I arrived. The few days I was able to spend in Alsace, I used in ordering supplies for the hospital. If war should really come, I must be at my post and be in charge at the hospital in the difficult situations which it would bring.

I again sailed into the River Ogowé on March 3, 1939. As we sailed between the wooded banks which loomed before us, I asked myself what would happen before I again came down the river to the sea. In the next months, I used all the hospital funds to purchase a supply of medicines, drugs, and other necessities. Some I bought in Africa; others had to come from Europe. Fortunately, almost all the supplies arrived before the outbreak of war. (73)

In March, 1940, the passenger boat *Brazza,* which had been running between Bordeaux and Equatorial Africa, was torpedoed in the vicinity of Cape Finisterre. The boat went down so quickly that only a few passengers were rescued. Many of those who died were from our region. . . . With the sinking of the ship, we lost our last consignment of materials from Europe. . . .

The startling events of May and June, 1940, convinced all of us that the war had really broken out and that it would not yield to the former in frightfulness but really surpass it.

In the fighting between the troops of General de Gaulle and those of Vichy which occurred in October and November, 1940, in the vicinity of Lambaréné, our hospital escaped damage. For this we had to thank both the location of the site as well as the respect of the contending forces. The hospital is not at Lambaréné itself but four kilometers upstream, and it is separated from it by a wide stream perhaps five hundred meters across. The crews of the airplanes on both sides were ordered not to bomb the hospital. It therefore became a place of refuge for both Europeans and Africans. We secured ourselves from stray gunfire by strengthening the walls of our houses which faced Lambaréné with heavy corrugated iron. Fortunately, we had enough of it available. (74)

The road which leads from Leopoldville to Brazzaville runs from Cape Town, through Lambaréné, to Algeria. There is a ferry over the arms of the Ogowé. About five hundred meters upstream from the hospital, the northern stretch of the road leading to the Cameroun and Nigeria begins. . . . One must be in control of this road in case it is too dangerous or too difficult to transport troops from south to north or from west to east by sea. (75)

In the summer of 1941, my wife arrived at Lambaréné. She had gone from France to Lisbon. From there she sailed on a Portuguese boat to the colony of Angola at the mouth of the Congo. Traveling through the Belgian Congo, she arrived at Lambaréné on August 2. (76)

During 1944 we became conscious of how really tired we were. This exhaustion is the result of our long work in the hot, damp equatorial climate and of continuous over-exertion in excessive work. We have to draw upon our last reserves of energy in order to be able to perform the tasks our work demands. Not to become ill, again to be able to go to work—this is our daily concern. How clear it is to all of us that, if someone is forced to give up, there is no possibility of another taking up his work. Substitutes can no longer come to our rescue. . . . Nevertheless, we remain erect.

While we are always exhausted, our work continues to exact more of us. A large measure of the additional work is due to the continually increasing number of European patients who must be hospitalized. . . . The real cause of these cases of ill health is, next to the tropical climate, diet deficiencies. . . .

In the shipments of medicines which we received from America, Europe, and Switzerland, there were arsenic, iron, and liver preparations which we need in the struggle against anemia. Thus many Europeans who come to us exhausted and pale leave the hospital in a somewhat satisfactory condition. (77)

Among the African patients we find, as before, many with phagedenic ulcers. . . . Heart difficulties are frequently met among the natives. Usually they come to us first when the malady has developed to the point where they have difficulty breathing or have dropsy. The excellent equipment which we received from Switzerland makes it possible for us to give help in most cases, even to those who come to us so late.

Many African patients come to us with rheumatism and sciatica. . . . Not infrequently there are stomach ulcers among the Africans. . . .

Tuberculosis is found here. The cases of lung tuberculosis have as a rule an uninterrupted, unfortunate course. Among cases of bone tuberculosis, we often see illnesses of the breast vertebra, which frequently respond well to treatment. There is also intestinal tuberculosis among the Africans. . . .

There are far fewer cases of sleeping sickness now than in the early years, because a government health program is directed at it in our region. . . . As in the early days, we have to cope with leprosy among the natives. . . . Recently there has appeared a real hope of coming medically to grips with it. (78)

Although we are not constantly on the run, we are always preoccupied and oppressed by what we fear will come to pass. We feel ashamed that we have enough to eat here, while millions at a distance suffer from hunger. The news of those who are in prison camps, of the abuse of the Jews, and of the suffering which is endured by displaced people fills us with horror. . . . We know that we must seize courage from one another daily in order to go forward in the face of depression with the work which is given us to do. It continually strikes us as incomprehensible that we are called to a work of mercy, while others are condemned to suffering or must commit deeds which result in injury or death. This blessing daily gives us new energy for our tasks and makes them precious to us. (79).

The news of the war's end came at midday on Monday, May 7. . . . In the afternoon, the hospital bell was rung and the community gathered to hear the good news. Later, in spite of great fatigue, I had to drag myself to the plantation to see how the work there was progressing.

Only in the evening did I have an opportunity to reflect on the significance of the end of hostilities in Europe and what it must mean to many men to be able, after some years, to experience their first night without fear of bombardment. (80)

Considering the great impoverishment which has set in everywhere but is not always visible, doubt invades us as to whether from now on the further extension of our work will be possible.

We have faith, however, that the friends of our

work will remain true to it under the coming difficult conditions. One thing is certain—this work is necessary, as necessary in the future as it has been in the past. Those of us who know how much physical suffering exists here and how much the hospital does for the many who suffer venture to ask our friends: "Help, that we may continue to help them in the future." (81)

IN THE UNREST OF THE TIME

In 1921 I had the pleasure of playing the organ at the first performance of Bach's St. Matthew Passion at the Orféo Català. It was the first time that this work was performed in Spain.

I resigned my two positions in Strasbourg in April, 1921, to support myself by my organ playing. In order to work undisturbed on my *Philosophy of Culture,* I moved with my wife and child—a daughter born to us on my birthday, January 14, 1919—to my father's parsonage in Günsbach. In Strasbourg, where I frequently spend long periods of time working in the library, I rented an attic room. . . .

My work was, of course, frequently interrupted by journeys. I received invitations from different universities to lecture on the philosophy of culture or on the problems of primitive Christianity. I also had to deliver lectures about the hospital at Lambaréné in order to raise funds for carrying on the work there. By organ concerts, I provided for the support of my family and myself during the years I would be in Africa.

In the autumn of 1921, I was in Switzerland. In November I went from there to Sweden. Leaving Sweden at the end of January, I went to Oxford in order to deliver the Dale Memorial Lectures in Mansfield College. After that I lectured in the Selly Oak College at Birmingham . . . and at Cambridge. I also gave a series of organ concerts in England. (82)

For the most part, my audience was made up of missionaries or those preparing for mission work, that is, Christians who would have to vindicate Christianity before other world religions, especially Buddhism and Hinduism. In my lectures, I tried to clarify what was unique and peculiarly profound about Christianity. (83)

From the Lectures in England: You and I desire to preach the Christian gospel in the world. Consequently, it is essential that we be clear why it is for us the highest wisdom. Why do we think it to be the leaven which will leaven the thought, will, and hope of all humanity?

In our time, it is especially necessary that our thinking be clear on this issue. Today men are making a searching examination of religiosity in the world generally. . . . Is simple Christianity really the deepest expression of man's religious yearnings? Now do not expect me to voice an apology of the kind we generally meet before such a question—an apology which contends that Christianity contains truths which are above all reason and which, therefore, do not have to be made commensurate with reason. This looks to me like a retreat to a mountain fortress, which is excellent for defense, but from which one cannot launch a vigorous offensive.

From my youth I have been convinced that all religious truth must be conceived as truth which can necessarily be understood. In the field where ideas struggle with one another and where religions enter into contest with one another, Christianity cannot plead for special treatment. It must be in the thick of the battle of ideas, trusting in the power of its inherent truth. (84)

When you preach the gospel, beware of proclaiming it as the religion which explains everything. I imagine that in England, as on the Continent, many thousands of men despair of Christianity because they have seen and experienced the abominations of war. In face of the inexplicable, the religion which they believed to be the explanation of everything collapsed.

For ten years before my departure for Africa, I taught boys in the confirmation classes of St. Nicholas' in Strasbourg. After the war, some of them came to me and thanked me for teaching them clearly that religion was not a formula for explaining everything. Whereas many in the trenches, not being prepared for the inexplicable, had thrown Christianity over, they were able to hold to it.

When you preach, therefore, lead men away from the desire to know everything to the one thing that is necessary, namely, the desire to be in God, through which we become other than the world and through which we are redeemed from the world, standing beyond all riddles. "If I have only you, I ask nothing from heaven and earth." "All things work together for good to them that love God." These insights are the peaks of Ararat, where men may find refuge when the flood of the inexplicable sweeps over all else. (85)

In the middle of March, 1922, I returned to Sweden from England in order to give more concerts and lectures. Scarcely had I returned, when I left again to present lectures and concerts in Switzerland.

In the summer of 1922, I was able to work undisturbed on the *Philosophy of Culture.*

In the autumn I went back to Switzerland. After that I lectured on ethics at Copenhagen at the invitation of the theological faculty there. There were also organ concerts and lectures in various towns in Denmark.

In January, 1923, at the invitation of Professor Oscar Kraus, I lectured at Prague on the philosophy of culture. . . .

Early in 1923 the first two volumes of the *Philosophy of Culture* were finished. They appeared in the same year. (86)

From the Preface of the Second Volume, "Culture and Ethics": My subject is the tragedy of the western world-view.

Even as a student I was surprised that the history of thought was presented always as a history of philosophical systems, not as a history of the struggles to achieve a world-view. Later, when reflecting on the cultural movement in which I stood, I was struck by the strange and unyielding relations which exist between culture and world-view. I felt impelled to direct to western thought the question as to what it had sought and what it had achieved as regards a world view. What remains of our philosophical achievements, when they are stripped of their sham scholarship? What do they offer us when we ask for the basic sustenance we need in order to live as vital, profound, and humane persons?

Thus I gave myself to an unsparing analysis of western thought. (87)

In this book I have written, therefore, about the tragedy of the search for a world-view. I have here also moved along a new path to a proper world-view. . . . It is my faith that, if the requisite revolution is to occur, we must exercise ourselves as thinking men.

A new renaissance must come—one much greater than that into which we stepped out of the Middle Ages. It must be a renovation in which mankind discovers that the ethical is the highest truth and the highest practicality. In it mankind must experience liberation from that impoverished understanding of reality by which it has up to now been chained.

As a humble herald of this renaissance, I proclaim a faith in a new humanity, casting it as a torch into the darkness of our age. I dare to do this, because I believe I can offer a philosophy of life as a firm foundation for the movement to humanity, which until now has subsisted only as a noble sentiment. This philosophy of life is a result of elemental thinking and encompasses a generally intelligible world-view. It and the movement of humanity it stimulates achieve a new power of attraction and persuasion. Moreover, its worth can now be assessed by testing its conclusions in an energetic and consistent manner against reality. (88)

From the vain endeavor to unite a knowledge of the world and ethics into a world-view, human thought must turn to the task of drawing forth the world-view of ethics. (89)

How magnificent life was in those years! When I went to Africa, I was ready to make three sacrifices: to abandon the organ; to forsake teaching, in which I had invested my heart; and to give up my financial independence, relying for the rest of my life on help from friends.

I had begun to make these sacrifices. Only my close friends knew how difficult it was for me.

But now the miracle which came to Abraham as

he prepared to sacrifice his son occurred for me. I too was spared from making the sacrifice. I was permitted to continue my work on the organ, because the Paris Bach Society gave me a piano with pedal attachment, built for the tropics, and because my health won a victory over the tropical climate. . . . When I returned to Europe, I did so, not as one who had degenerated into an amateur, but as an artist in full possession of his powers. Moreover, I discovered that I was more esteemed as an artist now than before.

In place of the teaching duties at Strasbourg University, which I had forsaken, there were many lectures for me to give in various universities.

Having lost my financial independence for a season, I was now able to win it back by organ and pen.

To be relieved of the necessity of making the three-fold sacrifice was an encouraging experience which, in all the trials that fell upon me, has kept me strong and ready for every effort and for every renunciation. (90)

The future of humanity depends upon each person striving, in whatever situation he finds himself, to manifest true humanity to men.

In any moment of inactivity, great values are left unrealized through neglect. Whenever they are willed and enacted, they constitute a wealth which should not be underestimated. Our humanity is not so materialistic that it will always be expressed in idle talk. As I have come to know men, it has become clear to me that many more idealistic desires are present among them than become visible. Just as the waters of the visible stream are small in comparison to those which flow underground, so is also the discernible idealism among men in comparison with that which is unreleased or just barely expressed in their hearts. (91)

GOETHE

From the Goethe Prize Address, Delivered at Frankfort-am-Main, August 28, 1928

At the end of my days as a student, I reread by chance the description of the *Harzreise* in the winter of 1777. It struck me as wonderful that this man, whom we consider an Olympian, made his way through November mists and rain in order to visit and to try to bring spiritual help to a pastor's son who was in spiritual distress. Again I discovered in the Olympian a profoundly simple man. I learned to love Goethe. Thus, when I had to render help to some man in the course of my life, I said myself, "This is your Harzreise."

When life's way led me to undertake a work far removed from my natural talents and distant from the vocation for which I had prepared, Goethe the comforter provided the words to help me. Even those who best understood me found fault with my decision to study medicine. I was not really prepared for this, they said. It was quixotic. I reflected that this venture would not perhaps have appeared so quixotic to the great man who permitted his Wilhelm Meister to become a surgeon in order to serve, although he was not prepared for it. And it struck me as something significant for all of us that Goethe, in his endeavor to understand human destiny, permits Faust and Wilhelm Meister to end their lives in thoroughly humble activities, through which they achieve humanity in the fullest sense.

As I began to prepare myself for this new vocation and service, I met Goethe again. In preparation for my medical career, I had to study natural science. I did it as a student but he as a man of research. How remote the natural sciences were from the intellectual achievements I planned before I entered my practical work! Then I remembered that Goethe had come back into the natural sciences from intellectual activities. It disturbed me that he lost himself in the natural sciences at the time when so much of what moved within him should have been given its final form. Now I was required to devote myself to the natural sciences, although my preoccupation had formerly been with intellectual matters. By this fortune I was, however, required to sound the depths of my nature. I discovered why Goethe surrendered himself in loyalty to natural sciences. It is a distinctive gain and an occasion of enlightenment for anyone immersed in intellectual work to confront facts which are to be reckoned with, not because he has imagined them, but simply because they exist. All thinking is strengthened when, forsaking preoccupation with imagined entities, it must work its way through reality. And when I experienced this "necessity of working one's way through reality," I was able to view the man who had made this movement before all of us.

When my trying student days had passed and I ventured forth as a doctor, I met Goethe again. This time I conversed with him in the primeval forest. I had thought that I would go there as a doctor. In my early years, I let those who, in my opinion, were fitted for or hired for manual labor do it. Soon, however, I recognized that this could not be. Either they did not put in an appearance or they were not qualified to handle the job well. Therefore, I undertook work which was quite different from my medical duties. But the worst was yet to come. In the last months of 1925, a great famine threatened the hospital. In order to protect against such a threat in the future, I set to work establishing a plantation for the hospital. I directed the clearing of the site myself. . . . For weeks and months I stood in the jungle, harassed by obstinate workers, trying to turn forest into fruitful land. When I was overwhelmed with despair, I thought of Goethe, who had his Faust busy at the end redeeming the land from the sea in order that men might live and find nourishment there. In the dark primeval forest, Goethe stood beside me as a smiling and understanding comforter.

One other thing I owe to Goethe; and I must mention it. A deep concern for justice infused him. At the turn of the century, theories arose which contended that what was to be achieved should be done without regard to the right and without regard to the fate of the men affected by the change. I did not know how these theories, which had their impact on all of us, were to be met. It was a most meaningful experience, then, to find in Goethe the ardent desire to do what had to be done without sacrificing the right. Whether in Europe or Africa, I read the last pages of Faust at Easter, and I am deeply moved by them. They tell of Faust's last guilty act in which he determines to get rid of the hut which stands in his way by a slight, well-intentioned act of violence. He says he is tired of justice. But the well-intentioned act becomes a frightening deed by which lives are lost and by which the hut goes up in flames. The addition of this episode at the end of Faust gives us an insight into Goethe. How deep was his concern for justice and how profound his longing to accomplish things without injuring others!

My final, enduring experience of Goethe resulted from the vital way in which he participated in the life of his time, its thoughts and its events. The currents of the time moved through the stream of his consciousness. This is the striking thing about, not only the young Goethe and the mature Goethe, but also the old Goethe. When the mail coach used to creep along the road and the industrial age seemed only a shadow before most of us, the industrial age was already present for him. He was busy with the problems of the replacement of human labor by machines. If he is no longer master of his material in *Wilhelm Meister's Travels,* it is not because he no longer possesses the creativity he once had but because the material has developed into something immeasurable and intractable. He is trying to infuse this material with his whole experience and his deep concern for the future. Among the men of his time, he attempts to be a person who comprehends the coming new era and will match his powers with it. This is what deeply impresses one about the old Goethe.

In such encounters as these, I came to know Goethe intimately. He does not fill one with enthusiasm. In his work he advances no new, inspiring theories. He offers us what he has experienced in thought and action and what he has transformed into a higher reality. Only in personal experience do we come near to him. Only through an experience commensurate with his do we find him a friend instead of a stranger. We thus feel ourselves united to him in reverent friendship.

Before us, Goethe lived through the anxieties and

labors of this era. The conditions of modern life have become more chaotic than even he could foresee with his clear vision. Our strength must be greater than that of the circumstances of our life, if we are truly to become men, men who understand their situation and are a match for it.

Goethe's spirit places upon us three obligations. We must contend with the conditions of modern life so that men, who are about to have their humanity strangled by their work, may be able to preserve and enhance their spiritual lives. We must contend with men so that, in a time when external things make so great an impact on their lives, they can find the way to inwardness and persevere in it. And we have to wrestle with ourselves and with everyone else so that, in a time of confusion and inhumanity, we can remain true to the great humane ideals of the eighteenth century, translating them into the concepts of our day and advancing their realization.

In his own life and in his own calling, each must undertake this task in the spirit of the great child of Frankfort, whose birthday we celebrate today in his birthplace. He does not recede from us with the passage of time but moves closer. As we move forward, we recognize Goethe more clearly as a man who, by a deep and comprehensive experience, was concerned for and worked for his age. We too must become persons who understand our time and are a match for it.

Goethe accomplished all these things with the priceless gifts which fortune here laid in his cradle. Our obligation is to act like men who have received only one small pound but who want to be faithful in our stewardship. Let it be so! (92)

For Goethe, while the ethical is a universal value, it finds expression in an individual or concrete way. He himself sought to express this in living to the achievement of nobility. For him the true good was to impart truth, purity, and peace. One cannot deny that this was his aspiration and that it was achieved only in a limited degree. Whoever has probed his life is struck by the way in which he persevered in bringing to fulfillment the truth, sincerity, and peacefulness rooted in him. Never did Goethe react in kind to the many open and concealed hostilities which he met. He went his way amid all these assaults quietly and peacefully.

The tremendous purity! He always goes his way. He is reproached for not having enough understanding of active love or for lacking enthusiasm. But whereas the light of active love shows itself by a feeble gleam, it burns inwardly by a deep flame. He possessed a love which was peculiarly his own.(93)

Resignation is part of Goethe's world-view. A person should not act in the interests of the results but simply from an inner necessity. He once expressed this thought beautifully with reference to a parable of Jesus. The true man who has a work to do is like the man in the parable who sows seed about him without observing where and how it falls. This is how he understands the parable. (94)

Although Goethe left behind him no completed world-view, he remained true to himself. He gave us, however, a confession of faith in a view of life which he, finite man that he was, tried to realize in his life.

The greatness of a thinker rests in the unity of life and thought which he has achieved. We find this in Goethe. . . . No one who comes to Goethe goes away empty-handed. He takes away something of value for his life. (95)

To men of all times, Goethe's prophetic message is: "Strive for true humanity!"

JOHANN SEBASTIAN BACH

The peculiar thing about Bach is that he did not try to gain recognition for his greatest works and he did not ask the world to become acquainted with them. Hence the spirit of consecration which surrounds his works. In his cantatas, we sense a kind of virginal charm which we do not meet in other art-works. The gray volumes of the old Bach Society speak a moving language. They tell us of something that will not be lost, because it is true and great and was created not in order to gain recognition, but because it had to be created.

Bach's cantatas and passions are not merely the offspring of the Muse. They are also the children of leisure,* in the honorable and profound sense which this term had in times gone by when it sig-

* . . . sind nicht nur Kinder der Muse, sondern auch Kinder der Musse. . . .

nified the hours of life which a man used for himself and himself alone.

Bach was not aware of the uniqueness and greatness of his work. . . . He stands perhaps highest among creative artists. His creative energies expressed themselves without self-consciousness, as do those in nature. They are, therefore, as elemental and enriching as the latter. (96)

The master's artistic activity and personality are rooted in his piety. If he is to be understood at all, it must be from this perspective. For him, art was religion. It had no concern with the world and success in worldly affairs. It was an end in itself. According to Bach, religion is included in the definition of art in general. All great art, even if it is called secular, is really religious from his point of view. For him the tones do not fade away—they rise as an ineffable praise to God. (97)

In his inner being, Bach belongs to the history of German mysticism. (98)

Viewed from without, Bach's life seems a scene of conflict and bitterness. In reality, it was, however, peaceful and serene. (99)

As death neared, he dictated to Altnikol (who became his son-in-law in 1749) a chorale fantasia on the melody, "Wenn wir in höchsten Nöten sein," and told him to head it with the opening of the hymn, "Vor deinen Thron tret ich allhier," which is sung to the same melody. In the manuscript, we can see all the pauses the sick man had to make.

The drying ink is more watery from day to day. The notes written at twilight, with the windows curtained, are scarcely readable.

With the veil of death descending, Bach wrote this piece in a dark room. It is unique among his creations. No description can do justice to the perfection of its contrapuntal art. Each segment of the melody is presented in a fugue, in which the inversion of the theme figures each time as the countertheme. The flow is so natural that after the second line we are not conscious of the art but are completely caught up in the spirit which speaks through these G major harmonies. The storms and confusions of the world no longer penetrated the curtained windows. Around the dying master the harmonies of the spheres sounded. No sorrow invades the music. The peaceful quavers move on the far side of all human passion. Over the whole shines the word "Transfiguration." (100)

In contrast to the Bach of those guardians of the grail of pure music, I present the Bach who is a painter and poet in music. He sets forth in vital clarity all the emotional and pictorial content of the text. Above all he is intent on interpreting the pictorial in lines of tones. He is really more of a tone painter than a tone poet. His art is closer to that of Berlioz than to that of Wagner. If the text tells of shifting mists, of raging winds, of rushing rivers, of waves that rise and fall, of falling leaves, or bells that ring to register death, of firm faith or of weak faith, of the proud who are exalted, of Satan's threats, or of angels from heaven's heights—Bach makes us see and hear all these in his music.

Bach commands a language of sound. His music is a vehicle of recurring rhythmical motives, voicing peaceful happiness, living joy, intense pain, or misery sublimely met.

The drive to express poetic and pictorial thoughts is the essence of music. Music is an invitation to the creative imagination of the hearer to make alive the feelings and the visions from which it derived. But this can only come to pass, if he who speaks in the language of sound possesses the mysterious capacity of rendering thought clearly and vividly. On this point, Bach is the greatest among the great.

His music is poetic and pictorial because its themes are born of poetic and pictorial ideas. From these themes, the composition is developed, an architectural structure of lines of tones. The pictorial and poetic music reveals itself as Gothic architecture in sound. The greatest thing about the elemental vitality, majestic plasticity, and structural perfection we find in Bach's music is the spirit which permeates the whole. In this music a soul which seeks for peace amid the world's unrest and has, indeed, already tasted this blessing permits others to share its experience. (101)

Even to his death, he deviated only in the most limited way from his poetic interpretation of music and from his language of tones. The language of the cantatas is the same as that of the *Orgelbüchlein.* (102)

The *Orgelbüchlein* is not only of significance in the story of the development of the chorale prelude, but it is itself one of the greatest events in music. Never before had anyone expressed the texts in pure music in this way. No one afterwards attempted to do so by such simple means. . . . The *Orgelbüchlein* is, therefore, the dictionary for Bach's language of tones. (103) Suddenly it appears, complete and perfect. (104) If we are to understand what is expressed in the themes of the cantatas and passions, we must begin with it. Until the significance of the *Orgelbüchlein* was perceived, the fundamental character of Bach's music remained dark and debatable. (105)

Bach's music is Gothic. In such architecture, the overall plan is born of a simple motive, reveals itself in rich detail rather than rigid line, and comes alive through the vividness and clarity of the details. So it is with Bach's music. The impression it makes on the listener depends upon the player's communicating the encompassing plan and the details together in a clear and living manner.

If we replace this double architectonic dynamic by the unary emotional dynamic, such as we have in Beethoven's works, we have simply done our best to make Bach unintelligible, mixing the great and the small nuances into one. (106)

The Brandenburg concertos are the purest revelation of Bach's polyphonic style. Neither on the organ nor on the clavier could he have worked out the architectonic structure of a piece with such vitality. The orchestra alone permits absolute freedom in the employment and grouping of obbligato voices. . . . We see before us what the philosophy of all ages depicts as the elemental mystery of existence, namely, the self-unfolding of the idea, in which it creates its own opposite, struggles to overcome it, and proceeds thus until it returns to itself, having traversed the whole of existence. One experiences the same incomprehensible necessity and mysterious satisfaction when he follows the theme of one of these concertos, from its opening in the *tutti,* through its puzzling struggle with its opposite, to its self-realization in the final *tutti.* (107)

Are the Brandenburg concertos suitable for our concert halls? . . . These works are destined to become popular possessions in the same sense as the Beethoven symphonies are. (108)

The declamatory unity of tone and word in Bach is like that in Wagner. In the latter it is self-evident since the verbal phrase is musically conceived, the music adding only the intervals. In Bach, the unity is displayed in a more inspiring manner. The tones give the words more vitality. The music purges them of lowly connotations. They are revealed in their true form. This miracle occurs repeatedly in the cantatas and the passions. As a result, we take it as a commonplace. As we penetrate deeply into Bach, however, we repeatedly experience the ever-new and ever-greater astonishment which a thoughtful man feels in those daily events which are at the same time the greatest wonders. (109)

The effect of Bach's music rests, not in the perfection of the presentation, but in its spirit. Mendelssohn, Schelble, and Mosewius, who were the first to resurrect the cantatas and passions, were able to do so because they were profound and feelingful men as well as musicians. Only he who sinks himself in Bach's emotional world, who lives and thinks with him, and who is as simple and modest as he, can rightly bring Bach's music to the listener. If the director and the performer are not consecrated in thought and mood, they cannot communicate effectively to the hearer. There is something cold about the music. It is drained of its best power. Perhaps now more than ever before, we need that "one necessary thing" of which Mosewius spoke in 1845, when he was trying to interest the world in Bach's cantatas. This understanding must prevail. Then Bach can help our time achieve that spiritual unity and depth which it needs so desperately. (110)

Bach is an objective artist. The work of the objective artist is not impersonal; it is superpersonal. It is as if he felt but a single impulse, namely, to display definitively in a unique perfection what he finds in life. It is not he who lives—the spirit of the time lives in him. All the artistic movements, desires, creations, aspirations, and errors of his own generation and of the previous ones are comprehended and worked out in him.

In this respect, the greatest German musician can be compared only with the greatest German philosopher. Kant's work reveals the same impersonal character. He is only the intellect in which the philosophical ideas and problems of his time move to a conclusion. He uses without embarrassment the previously established scholastic terminology, just as Bach took over without examination the musical forms which his time offered him.

Bach is clearly not a single, concrete personality; he is a universal personality. He shared in the musical development of three or four generations. If we look at the story of this family, which had such a striking position in Germany's artistic life, we feel that everything which moves there must be actualized in something complete. It appears self-evident that one day a Bach must come in whom all those other Bachs will live again and forever and in whom the portion of German music incarnate in this family will find its fulfillment. Johann Sebastian Bach is, to use Kant's language, a historical postulate.

Any path we take through the poetry and music of the Middle Ages leads to him. (111)

Bach is an end. Nothing comes from him. Everything simply leads to him. To recite his true biography is to reveal the nature and development of German art, which is fulfilled and perfected in him. It relates also the strivings and failures of that art. This genius was no individual spirit but a corporate spirit. Centuries and generations have worked toward this end, before whose greatness we stand transfixed in reverence. Whoever has studied the history of this time and perceives its end recognizes that it is the realization of spirit before it objectified itself in a single personality. (112)

Nowhere as well as in the *Well-tempered Clavichord* do we come to understand that, for Bach, art was religion. He does not delineate natural psychic phenomena as Beethoven does in his sonatas. He does not exhibit a striving or struggling for a good. On the contrary, he reveals the reality of life as it is felt by a spirit which recognizes itself as superior to life and in which the conflict of emotions, the wildest grief, and the unrestrained cheerfulness are but aspects of a strong, triumphant core of being. This is the spirit of the sorrow-laden E flat minor prelude of the First Part and the carefree, vital prelude in G major of the Second Part. Whoever has felt this marvelous peace has understood the mysterious spirit which has here translated its world-view into the secret language of tone. He will thank Bach as one renders thanks to those great spirits who reconcile men with life and bring them peace. (113)

THE UNKNOWN ONE*

Only those to whom it has been disclosed that all help, improvements and benefits must be directed to the creation of a new spirit really understand the nature of work in our time. Work which is not done to this end is a road to uncertainty! The spirit in which we work is the spirit of Jesus. (114)

To the participants in the Conference of the International Society for Free Christianity in Bern:

Lambaréné, Sunday, August 10, 1947

Let me say how sorry I am not to be able to be present at the Conference. For different reasons, it

* In the rich spiritual life of this remarkable man [Schweitzer], the character and ethics of Jesus is the dominant note. Jesus' personality and life-view are his, even though the metaphysics of the Nazarene is far different from his own. Though it is certain that Schweitzer's ethical achievement is the most praiseworthy of all the many activities which constitute his inner life . . . , it is also certain that the similarity of his motives to those of Jesus, which he often accents, is the most noteworthy aspect of his psychological personality. (Oscar Kraus, *Albert Schweitzer* [Prague, 1929], p. 51.)

is impossible for me to travel to Europe now. Nevertheless, I am with you in thought this day.

In this Conference, do not hide from the fact that you serve an unpopular cause! Liberal Christianity is as unpopular today as it ever has been, because the dominant spirit of our time attempts to smother liberal religious thinking. On the other hand, it is a timely cause—as timely as ever—because it is a necessity for the spiritual life of our age. Only through a renewal of ethical and religious thought can the spirit arise which imparts to mankind the knowledge and power necessary for the pilgrimage from darkness and strife to light and peace. Liberal Christianity has the magnificent responsibility of communicating and upholding the conviction that thought and religion are not incompatible but belong together. Every deep piety is reflective; every really deep thought is reverent.

The greatest spirits among men have endeavored to unite thought and religion, because they judged it necessary for the spiritual welfare of man. In a time which must achieve reverence for spiritual truth, we carry on this effort. For us, the nuclear doctrine of Christianity is the kingdom of God. Only a Christianity which is animated and ruled by the idea and the intent of the kingdom of God is genuine. Only such a Christianity can give to mankind what it so desperately needs.

As we speak for liberal Christianity and expect men to arrive at religious positions by their own thinking, we have before us the image of Jesus, who insisted that one should not, in the name of religion, place on men's shoulders improper and heavy burdens. We also hold to the words of Paul: "Where the spirit of the Lord is, there is liberty."

May your liberal Christianity prove effective in spirit and deed in accomplishing its task in our day. May we all stay awake to the necessity of working to the end that our piety becomes deeper and more vital and that the power of Jesus' spirit flows through us. Our ideal is not merely liberal Christianity but the most profound Christianity. (115)

"Autumn has arrived in church dogmatics, because the sun of the kingdom of God no longer sheds its light there."

In ancient and medieval times, Christians had no faith in progress. They had no will to progress; they did not even entertain the idea that things could move ahead and upward. They did not sense that they were in an unnatural situation inasmuch as their faith and piety were founded on the idea that the kingdom of God was an event in the distant future. It was self-evident that the only possible attitude toward things concerning this kingdom was a passive one.

Things are different with modern men who have been influenced by the spirit of life-affirmation and world-affirmation. To them it is obvious that the kingdom of God is an ethical and spiritual event which is to be conceived as developing in this world and which requires the ethical efforts of believers for its realization. (116)

Those who have the courage to let the texts of Matthew and Luke mean what they say must agree that Jesus' view of the kingdom of God belongs in the framework of late Jewish eschatology. He did not spiritualize it. As a matter of fact, he used it as a means for expressing his powerful and profound ethic of love.

Of course, it is hard for us to admit that Jesus, who is uniquely an expression of God's spirit and is the supreme revealer of religious and spiritual truth, did not stand above his time in the manner in which his universal significance suggests he should have.

Men of every age would prefer to find in Jesus a highest kind of religious knowledge which is unchanging and simple to acquire. But now we see that he shared the views of an age which are for us untrue and unacceptable. . . . Can he any longer be an authority for us?

I have suffered much from having to advance a truth which must be offensive to Christian faith.

For me, however, Jesus remains what he was. Not for a minute did I have to struggle for my faith that in him we find the highest spiritual and religious authority. Nevertheless, he was in error in expecting an early coming of a supernatural kingdom of God. We cannot make such a hope ours. . . .

We must assume a limitation of knowledge in Jesus. We cannot suppose that, although he possessed a knowledge of nature and its happenings equal to that acquired, or possible of acquisition, by modern science, he simply refrained from using it. The historical Jesus partook in a normal manner of the outlook of his time. There was no pretense here on his part. The limitations of his knowledge were realities. Anything else would be an interpretation which did him an injustice.

If Jesus understood the world and its occurrences in terms of the outlook of his day, then his interpretation of the coming of the kingdom of God must be similar to that of late Judaism.

Anyone who studies the way in which progress is achieved in history sees clearly that something entirely new does not easily establish itself. If perchance it does succeed in getting a footing, it is likely to seem unnatural and questionable. Thus, even if Jesus had held a completely spiritualized interpretation of the kingdom of God and its coming, his preaching about it would have been very difficult to believe. . . .

Now Jesus did spiritualize the conception of the kingdom of God insofar as he subjected it to his ethic of love. In time, then, this ethic brought about a renovation of the concept of the kingdom of God. . . .

The fact that Jesus conceived the realization of the kingdom in a way that was refuted by fact does not call into question his authority as a unique revealer of spiritual insights. It only refutes the conventional interpretation of his authority and personality. Under the influence of Greek metaphysics, faith ascribed to him a divinity and a divine inerrancy to which he made no claim. . . . He is so great that the revelation that he belonged to his age cannot harm him. He remains our spiritual lord.

All attempts to escape the fact that Jesus entertained a conception of the kingdom and its early coming which was unfulfilled are flights from the truth. So are also all attempts to avoid the fact that this conception is inappropriate for us. In this respect, truth is the essence of the spiritual life. A faith which shuns obvious facts is an impoverished faith. . . .

The modern conception of the kingdom of God and its coming creates a spiritual situation which is like that of Jesus, his companions, and the Christians of the first generation. Now, after many centuries, there is a vital concern with the question of the kingdom. Men generally are changing their minds about its interpretation.

For modern faith, the beginning of the kingdom is discovered in Jesus and in the spirit which entered the world with him. . . .

We cannot believe, as did men of a former age, that the kingdom comes of itself at the end of time. For mankind today, it is a question of realizing the kingdom or perishing. The tragedy of the human situation requires us to invest ourselves earnestly in its realization.

This is the beginning of the end for mankind. Will men use the powers given into their hands by the knowledge and techniques of modern science for creative or destructive purposes? As long as man's capacity for destruction was limited, we could hope that reason would place limits on disaster. We cannot be so optimistic today. Our only hope is that the spirit of God will triumph in its wrestling with the spirit of the world.

The last petition of the Lord's Prayer once again possesses its original meaning in relation to us. It is a prayer for deliverance from the dominion of evil powers in the world. For us, these powers are not embodied in angelic beings revolting against God. No, they are at work in the minds of men, and they are no less real because they are present there! The first believers placed their hope solely on the kingdom, anticipating the end of the world. We do so also, but expect the end of the race.

The spirit shows us the signs of the time and interprets for us their meanings.

The belief in the kingdom of God is the most difficult demand Christian faith makes of us. We are asked to believe in what seems impossible, namely in the victory of the spirit of God over the spirit of the world. Our trust and hope is invested in the miracle which the spirit can produce.

But the miracle must occur in us before it occurs in the world. We dare not hope that by our efforts we can create the conditions of the kingdom in the world. We must certainly work for it. But there can be no divine kingdom in the world, if there is not one first of all in our hearts. The beginning of the kingdom is to be found in our determination to bring our every thought and deed under the dominion of the kingdom. Nothing will come to pass without inwardness. The spirit of God will only contend against the spirit of the world when it has triumphed over that spirit in our hearts. (117)

It is as if I were under commission to impart to men the message that piety is independent of the traditional forms of faith. *(In a letter of the year 1954.)*

The Sermon on the Mount is the unassailable charter of liberal Christianity. By the authority of Jesus, the truth that the essence of religion is ethical is established.

Moreover, due to the withering of the late Jewish eschatological world-view, Jesus' religion of love has been freed from the dogmatism in which it was clothed.

The mold into which the casting was poured is shattered.

Now we are free to let the religion of Jesus come alive in our thought in its direct spiritual and ethical character. We know that much which is valuable has been carried to us in ecclesiastical Christianity, garbed in Greek dogmas and kept alive by the piety of many centuries. We, therefore, hold to the church in love, reverence, and gratitude.

But while hers, we are men who appeal to the words of Paul, "Where the spirit of the Lord is, there is freedom," believing that we serve Christianity better by our devotion to Jesus' religion of love than by submitting to all the articles of faith. If the church possesses the spirit of Jesus, there is ample room in her for every form of Christian piety, even for that which will be free. (118)

The victory of a liberal interpretation of religion does not by any means depend on whether it finds support in history but only on whether it maintains and develops its sense for truth and reality and proceeds on the path which leads to its goals. . . . The time is coming when, after a period in history in which men were preoccupied with the religious spirit unto itself, both thought and history are awarded their proper places and reconciled with one another in the assessment of religion. This can come to pass only if we become conscious of our real relationship to the past and of our freedom from it. Moreover, we must recognize that religion is founded not only on tradition and its significance but also, and indeed much more so, on the spirit. Only the spirit makes it possible to contend against authoritarian religiosity and to achieve through knowledge and deed, the victory of liberality of mind in its noblest and deepest sense. (119)

I have remained old fashioned in my method insofar as I present thoughts in their historically conditioned forms. It seems to me that today our ways of examining religious issues are so multifarious and so often shot through with dazzling virtuosity that the resulting confusion has very little relation in the long run to historical religious knowledge or to our religious life. Still, I am persuaded that the abiding spiritual significance which the religious thought of the past has for us finds its greatest worth and vigor when we enter into that piety as it really was, not as we interpret it for ourselves. A Christianity which does not dare place historical truth in the service of spiritual truth is not internally sound, even if it appears outwardly strong. The reverence for truth as such, which must be a part of our faith if it is not to be impoverished, includes a respect for historical truth. (120)

Instead of struggling for the triumph of the ethical spirit of God, by which the individual, the community, and religious groups would be infused with a spirit which sustained them, mankind is surrendering the world to the dominion of the spirit of thoughtlessness, being satisfied with the stagnation or retreat of culture and abandoning the endeavor to rise to the heights of humanity. Those who see the course of events and are not so stunned by it that they cannot be urgently anxious about the future of the world are prepared to understand and appreciate what, apart from all the strangeness of his speech, the historical Jesus had to say to us. They comprehend with him, who in the thought forms of his day experienced a similar anxiety and despair, that we are redeemed from our present unfortunate, irreligious situation by a vital hope and desire for the kingdom of God. In such a faith and hope and in an unconquerable moral spirit, we find steadfastness, freedom, and peace. As in the case of Jesus, by this faith and the vital energy which flows from it, we spread abroad the conviction and commitment that the highest good is focused in the kingdom of God and that for it we must live.

The crucial thing is the enthusiastic and the heroic in the world-view which proceeds from the will to and faith in the kingdom of God. It is a spirit of vigorous heroism which is not impaired but rather strengthened by the circumstances of life. In a religion there is as much understanding of the historical Jesus as there is a possession of a feelingful faith in the kingdom of God. Where this relationship is broken or undiscerned, there remain only empty words and formulas. We possess only as much of him as is yielded in us through the testimony of the kingdom of God.

It is a question of understanding the will to will. . . .

His words translate themselves in a form which must be received in our framework of ideas. Many of them which seem strange at first glance become true for us in a deep and eternal sense, if we do not attempt to repulse the power of the spirit which speaks through them.

Moreover, what modern sensibilities generally feel to be offensive in him is no longer an occasion of disturbance, if he is known by the will to will. He had repudiated work, possessions, and many other things which we reckon as ethical goods. For him, they were not good in themselves, because they were outside the bounds of the kingdom of God. For us, however, relations have shifted, so that what once lay in the shadows now marches along in the light. Furthermore, we put them into the service of the kingdom and remain in harmony with it, because we consider the kingdom as the measure of all moral values. (121)

We must return to the point where we can again perceive the heroic in Jesus. (122)

There came a man to rule the world. He ruled to the ends of blessing and destruction, as history testifies. He destroyed the world into which he was born. . . . That he continues to reign as the unique master and single truth in a world whose continuation he had denied is the elemental phenomenon of the antithesis between spiritual and natural truth which lies at the foundation of all life. In him, it became history. (123)

The names by which men expressed their recognition of Jesus as an authoritative ruler—Messiah,

Son of Man, Son of God—have become historical parables for us. If he himself used these titles, it was a qualified expression of the fact that he understood himself as a master and ruler. We can discover no designation which really expresses what he is for us.

He comes to us as one unknown, nameless, just as in an ancient time, by the lakeside, he came to those men who knew him not. He speaks the same word to us: "Follow me!" He places us at the tasks which he must fulfill in our time. To those who obey him, wise or simple, he will reveal himself in the labors, conflicts, and miseries they will experience in communion with him. As an ineffable mystery, they shall come inwardly to know who he is. (124)*

* The characterization which Schweitzer gives of Jesus completes the portrait of Schweitzer himself. (O. Kraus, *op. cit.*, p. 51.)

REVERENCE FOR LIFE

What is reverence for life and how does it originate in us? If one clearly understands himself and his relations with the world, he must ever reflect on the novel which is fashioned from the many, perceptible elements of his consciousness and on the primal, immediate, and continually given elements of conciousness. Only in this way can he arrive at a rational world-view. . . . The immediate facts of human consciousness testify: "I am life which wills to live in the midst of life which wills to live." In every instant in which he reflects on himself and on the world about him, man senses himself as a will to live in the midst of wills to live.

As in my will to live there is a desire for a wider life and for the mysterious exaltation of the will to live which we call pleasure—and also a dread of annihilation and of the mysterious encroachment on the will to live which we call pain—so it is also in the will to live around me, whether it comes to clear expression or remains dormant. (125)

If a man affirms his will to live, he acts naturally and honestly. He simply enacts in conscious thought what he has already accomplished in instinctive thought. The beginning of thought comes when a man senses his existence as something unfathomably mysterious, not as something objectively given. Life-affirmation is the spiritual act in which a man begins to live reflectively and begins to give himself to his life with reverence in order to realize its true value. Life-affirmation is a deepening and an exaltation of the will to live. (126)

Reverence for life gives the fundamental principle of morals, namely, that the good consists in the preservation, enhancement, and exaltation of life and that the destruction, injury, and retardation of life is evil. (127)

The ethics of reverence for life is the ethics of Jesus, philosophically expressed, made cosmic in scope, and conceived as intellectually necessary.

The great error of earlier ethics is that it conceived itself as concerned only with the relations of man to man. The real question is, however, one concerning man's relations to the world and to all life which comes within his reach. A man is ethical only when life, as such, is holy to him, that is, the lives of plants and animals as well as the lives of men. Moreover, he is ethical also only when he extends help to all life that is in need of it. Only the universal ethics of the ever-expanding sense of responsibility for all life can be grounded in thought. The ethics of the relation of man to man is not something unto itself. It is only a particular application of universal ethics.

The ethics of reverence for life, therefore, includes within itself all that can be called love, devotion, compassion, joy, and endeavor.

The world is a dreadful spectacle of the will to live contending against itself. One existence asserts itself at the cost of another. One destroys another. (128)

All living creatures stand under this law of the self-estrangement of the will to live. Man repeatedly discovers that he can only preserve his life or certain other lives at the cost of annihilating yet other forms of life. If he holds to the ethic of reverence of life, he injures or destroys life only under a necessity which cannot be escaped. Never does such a man annihilate living forms from thoughtlessness. Insofar as he is a free being, he seeks out every opportunity of partaking of the blessedness of advancing and assisting life and of protecting it from misery and destruction. (129)

I am most pleased by the new means of treating sleeping sickness. Whereas before I had to stand by and watch this painful disease run its course, now I can contribute to the preservation of life. Even so, every time I have under the microscope the germs which cause this illness, I cannot avoid reflecting that, in order to preserve life, I have to destroy other life.

I will buy from the Africans a young fish eagle which they have caught on a sandbank. But then I have to decide whether to let it starve or daily kill so many small fish in order to keep it alive. I decided for the latter course. Every day, however, I am oppressed by the fact that I am responsible for the sacrifice of one life for another. (130)

The ethics of reverence for life arises from real thinking and brings men into a real and continuous relationship with reality.

At first glance it appears as if reverence for life may be something too general and unlively to be made the content of a living ethics. A thinker does not need to concern himself about whether his expressions sound lively enough but only whether they are true and properly express life. Whoever falls under the influence of the ethics of reverence for life will come to feel the fire which glows in what he might have considered unlively expressions. The ethics of reverence for life is the world-wide ethics of love. It is the ethics of Jesus.

It is also objected that it ascribes to the natural life too great a value. To this we can reply that the fault of previous ethics is to be found in its not having recognized life as such as mysteriously valuable. All spiritual life exists in the context of the natural world. Reverence for life permits the fusion of the natural life and the spiritual life. The man in the parable of Jesus did not save the soul of the lost sheep; he saved the whole sheep. By the energy of reverence for natural life, reverence for spiritual life is awakened.

The ethics of reverence for life seems especially strange because it makes no distinction in value between the higher and the lower forms of life, between the more worthwhile and the less worthwhile forms of life. It is fundamental to it to omit such distinctions.

To undertake to legislate on matters of value among living beings entails having to judge whether they seem to stand, according to our feeling, nearer to or farther from us men. This means that we are really using a completely subjective standard. Who of us knows what significance attaches to other living beings in themselves or in relation to the world?

If one makes such a distinction, it follows that there are worthless forms of life. To injure or destroy them means nothing. Among such worthless beings, we may find included, depending upon the circumstances, species of insects or primitive peoples.

To the truly ethical man all life is holy, even that which appears to us from the human standpoint as the lowest. He makes distinctions only under the force of necessity, namely, when he finds himself in situations where he must choose which life he must sacrifice in order to preserve the other. He knows that he must bear the responsibility for the sacrificed life. (131)

Since I was devoted from my youth to the protection of animal life, it was a special joy to me to recognize that the universal ethics of reverence for life, which so often is reckoned as sentimentalistic, is a duty which no thinking man can evade. When will it come to pass that public opinion no longer puts up with popular amusements which entail mistreating animals?

The ethics of reverence for life is also thought not to be "reasonable," but irrational and enthusiastic. It marks out no intelligently determined boundaries for the sphere of obligation but places upon man the responsibility for all life which is within his reach and compels him to extend help to it. (132)

Reverence for life is an inexorable creditor!

The movement of reverence for life includes the movements of world-affirmation and life-affirmation as well as the ethical. It is directed to the creation of values and to the enhancement of progress which serve to develop to a higher degree the material, spiritual, and ethical status of men and humanity. While unreflective world-affirmation and life-affirmation staggers around among ideals of and passions for knowledge, techniques, and power, reflective affirmations set up the spiritual and ethical fulfillment of man as the highest goal, from which all other ideals of progress derive their real value.

In ethical world-affirmation and life-affirmation we come upon a cardinal point which permits us to distinguish between real culture and unreal culture.

An unspiritual cultural darkness loses its power over us, when we are infused by the spirit of the ethical. We dare to look truth in the face, observing that the development of knowledge and techniques makes the achievement of real culture more difficult, not easier. The problem of the correlation of the spiritual and the material is solved for us. We know that we all must wrestle in the interests of humanity over the relations among men and must be concerned to bring the almost hopeless battle in which many find themselves due to unspiritual social relations to a felicitous end. (133)

World-affirmation and life-affirmation in themselves can only produce an incomplete and imperfect culture. But, if they are profound and ethical, the will to progress which proceeds from them possesses the requisite insight for distinguishing the more valuable and the less valuable and there results a culture which not only exhibits an advance in knowledge and techniques but one which will above all bring to men and mankind spiritual and ethical benefits. (134)

Two things cast their shadows over my life. One is the thought that the world is inexplicably mysterious and full of misery. The other is that I have been born in a time of the spiritual decadence of mankind. I am, however, competent for handling both through the ethics of world-affirmation and life-affirmation which proceeds from the idea of reverence for life. In this way my life has been given firm foundation and clear direction.

So I live and work in the world as one who, through thought, tries to promote inwardness and moral improvement among men. Reverence for life produces in me an unrest which the world does not know, but from it I receive a blessing which the world cannot give.

I am completely opposed to the spirit of this age, because it promotes the neglect of thought. . . .

Today there is not only a neglect of thought but an actual distrust or deprecation of it. The organized political, social, and religious groups of our time are bent on inducing the individual to take up uncritically ready-made beliefs rather than inviting him to work out for himself by thought his own convictions. A man who thinks for himself and therefore is free is a troublesome and strange being. There is no assurance that he will fit comfortably into their organizations. All organized groups today find their strength, not so much in the spiritual values of their ideas or of the people who are their members, but in achieving the highest possible degree of unity and exclusiveness. In this they find their strongest power and surest defense.

Throughout his life, modern man is the object of influences which are directed to the end of robbing him of trust in his own power of thought. The spirit of spiritual dependence, to which he is to surrender, is imbedded in everything he reads and hears. It is incarnate in the people he deals with. It lurks in the groups and associations of which he becomes a member. It threatens him in all the circumstances of his life. From all sides and in many ways, pressure is applied to convince him that the truths and trusts which he needs for life have already been manufactured by organizations which have rights over him. The spirit of the age never lets him become his own man. It strangles freedom. Again and again, beliefs are forced upon him in the same way in which commercial establishments which have sufficient money can put pressure on him through high-powered advertising to buy their shoe polish or soap tablets.

The spirit of the age forces modern man to doubt his own capacity for thought in order to make him submit to authority. He cannot resist these insistent influences, because he is overworked, distraught, and anxious. The many constraints within whose domain it is his lot to work conspire to make him believe that he is incapable of thinking for himself.

The continually increasing, huge mass of knowledge which he faces shatters his self-confidence. He can no longer assimilate all the new discoveries being proclaimed. Although he does not understand them, he must take them as matters of fact. Given this situation in face of scientific truth, he is confirmed in the feeling that in matters of thought his judgment is not to be trusted.

Thus the circumstances of modern life deliver

modern man over as a victim to the authoritarian spirit of our time.

The seed of skepticism has germinated. Modern man no longer possesses spiritual self-confidence. Behind his mask of self-assurance, there is really a profound lack of self-confidence. Although he has tremendous abilities in material matters, he is intellectually stunted, because he does not use his capacity for individual, free thinking. It is incomprehensible that our age, which has distinguished itself by its many achievements in knowledge and skills, could have descended to such spiritual depths that it abandoned thinking. (135)

In order to move from the meaninglessness, which has made us captives, to meaningfulness, there is no other way than that each come back to himself and that all of us reflect about the way in which our will to work and to progress is derived from a meaning which we ascribe to our life and to all life about us. . . . This self-reflection on the ultimate and the elemental is the unique, reliable standard. Only in the measure that work is justified on the ground of the meaningfulness of my life and other lives are my intentions and deeds meaningful and valuable. . . .

How much of a mockery it is when people are beset by so many troubles, when the passions of nations have reached such proportions and intensity, when unemployment, poverty, and hunger are so prevalent, when power deals so shamelessly and senselessly with the powerless, when mankind will flee any way from the right—how much of a mockery it is to advance anything so odd as a return to reflection on the meaning of life. But only from such reflection can the strength come which is able to do something to rectify these derangements and distresses. Apart from such reflection, one is destined to use doubtful and inadequate standards.

When in the spring, the gray of the pastures gives way to green, it is due to the millions of new young shoots which sprout up from the old roots. The renewal of thought which is essential for our time can be achieved only when the many reshape their sensitivities and ideals as a result of reflecting on the meaning of life and on the meaning of the world. (136)

The beginning of all valuable spiritual life is courageous faith in the truth and an open confession of it. . . .

Simple reflection on the meaning of life has a value in itself. If such reflection should again arise among us, the ideals rooted in vanity and passion which now flourish among the masses would wither and die. How greatly we could improve our present condition, if we would all give three minutes each evening to gazing in meditation into the infinite world of stars above or if we would reflect on the meaning of life and death as we partake in a funeral rather than engaging in thoughtless conversation as we follow behind the coffin! The ideals which rise from folly or passion and guide those who make public opinion and direct public affairs would have no more power over men, if they began to reflect about the infinite and finite, existence and decay, and thus learned to distinguish between true and false standards. (137)

Although the paths along which we travel toward the goal still lie in darkness, the direction we must go is clear. (138)

WORLD PEACE

Modern men generally contend vigorously that reason and morality are not to be read into national perspectives. . . . (139) It seems clear that in all of its movements nationalism concerns itself with the morbid working of the imagination of the masses rather than with things as such. It is resolute in advancing *Realpolitik.* It does not really represent a selective, scientific interpretation of internal and external politics, but exhibits an egoistic and enthusiastic spirit. The *Realpolitik* of nationalism is a dogmatic, idealized, and emotionally overexaggerated view of unilateral territorial and commercial interests. It fights for its claims, without having made an intelligent assessment of their real value. As if to call into question the worth of millions, modern states burden themselves with armaments by the billions. Out of concern for defense and the expansion of trade, such high taxes are imposed that the nation's ability to compete is more seriously threatened than its foes.

Realpolitik is, as a matter of fact, *Irrealpolitik,* because it makes the simplest questions unanswerable through the introduction of popular emotions. It puts commercial interests in the shop-window, while it keeps in stock the grandiose ideas of nationalism. . . . It is significant for understanding the diseased nature of *Realpolitik* to see that it seeks to conceal its real interests in every way by glittering ideals. The war for power is the war for right and for culture. The egoistic community of interests among the people is presented as friendly and congenial. Moreover, if an earlier period of history in the state appears to have been an era of enmity and strife, the façade of congeniality is built across the past. (140)

From the conclusion of the speech on the occasion of receiving the Nobel Peace Prize in Oslo on November 4, 1954: Today we await the first sign of the work of the spirit to which we must entrust ourselves. It consists in nothing else than that all nations begin to make reparation, as far as possible, for what they did to others in the last war. Many thousands of prisoners and displaced persons are still waiting to return to their homes. Others, unjustly judged by foreign authorities, wait for acquittal. These and many other injustices still require rectification.

In the name of all those who strive for peace, I

venture to ask all peoples to take the first step along a new path. Not one will have to sacrifice a part of the authority and power he needs for self-preservation and defense.

Thus, if we make a beginning in the liquidation of the terrible war behind us, some measure of trust may arise among nations. Trust is the working-capital for all undertakings, without which nothing of real value can be accomplished. It provides the condition for beneficial developments in all spheres.

In the creative atmosphere of trust, the equitable adjustment of the problems which arose from the two wars can be made.

I believe that I voice the thoughts and hopes of millions of men who live in anxiety and in fear of future wars. May my words reach those who live on the other side of the barrier in the same anxiety as we do. May they receive my words in the sense in which they are offered.

Let those who hold the fates of peoples in their hands be careful to avoid everything which may worsen our situation and make it more perilous. Let them take to heart the marvelous words of the Apostle Paul: "As much as lies in you, be at peace with all men." They have meaning, not only for individuals, but also for nations. In their endeavors to preserve peace among themselves, may nations go to the uttermost limits of possibility, so that the human spirit may have time to develop, to grow strong, and to act! (141)

The rise of a reflective, profound, ethical will to progress will turn us from our lack of culture and from its attendant miseries to genuine culture. Sooner or later the true, conclusive renaissance must dawn which brings peace to the world. (142)

Reverence for life includes an elemental concept of responsibility to which we must surrender ourselves. In it there are energies which compel us to a revision and ennoblement of our individual, social, and political views and actions. (143)

One's world-view is, therefore, the germ cell of all conceptions and convictions which are determinative for the behavior of individuals and of groups. (144)

Sources

Afr. G—Afrikanische Geschichten. 1938. By permission of Richard Meiner Verlag, Hamburg, A. & C. Black, Ltd., London, and Macmillan Co., New York.

B—Joh. Seb. Bach. 1947. By permission of Breitkopf and Härtel Verlag, Wiesbaden, A. & C. Black, Ltd., London, and Macmillan Co., New York.

CW—Das Christentum und die Weltreligionen. 1924. By permission of C. H. Beck Verlag, München, George Allen & Unwin, Ltd., London, and Macmillan Co., New York.

Ex—Excerpts from various communications.

Goe—Goethe: Vier Reden. 1950. 3rd ed. By permission of C. H. Beck Verlag, München, and Beacon Press, Boston.

H-Kn—Elly Heuss-Knapp, *Ausblick vom Münsterturm.* 1934.

Ind—Die Weltanschauung der indischen Denker. By permission of C. H. Beck Verlag, München, and Beacon Press, Boston.

Jb—Jahrbuch des Freien Deutschen Hochstifts. Frankfurt-am-Main, 1928.

KE—Kultur und Ethik (Kulturphilosophie II). 4th ed. By permission of C. H. Beck Verlag, München, A. & C. Black, Ltd., London, and Macmillan Co., New York.

KJ—Aus meiner Kindheit und Jugendzeit. By permission of C. H. Beck Verlag, München, George Allen & Unwin, Ltd., London, and Macmillan Co., New York.

Kph. I—Verfall und Wiederaufbau der Kultur (Kulturphilosophie I). 1925. 2nd ed. By permission of C. H. Beck Verlag, München, A. & C. Black, Ltd., London, and Macmillan Co., New York.

Lb—Mitteilungen aus Lambaréné I/II. 1925. By permission of C. H. Beck Verlag, München.

LD—Aus meinem Leben und Denken. 1932. By permission of Richard Meiner Verlag, Hamburg, and Holt, Rinehart and Winston, New York.

LJ—Geschichte der Leben-Jesu-Forschung. 1933. 5th ed. By permission of J. B. C. Mohr Verlag, Tübingen, A. & C. Black, Ltd., London, and Macmillan Co., New York.

Mess—Das Messianitäts- und Leidensgeheimnis. 1901. By permission of J. B. C. Mohr Verlag, Tübingen, and Dodd, Mead & Co., New York; and the Macmillan Co., New York.

MP—Die Mystik des Apostels Paulus. 1930. By permission of J. B. C. Mohr Verlag, Tübingen, A. & C. Black, Ltd., London, and Macmillan Co., New York.

Oslo—Das Problem des Friedens in der heutigen Welt. 1954. By permission of C. H. Beck, München,

A. &. C. Black, Ltd., London, and Harper and Bros., New York.

Par—Pariser Rede von 1952 in Fischer-Bücherei "Genie der Menschlichkeit." 1955.

SRVbl—Schweizerisches Reform. Volksblatt. 1947.

SThU—Schweizerische Theologische Umschau, 1953.

Str. A—24 Aufsätze zur Jahrhundertwende, "Die Philosophie und die allgemeine Bildung in neunzehnten Jahrhundert." 1900. Kommissionsverlag der Strassburger Druckerei und Verlagsanstalt.

Tgb—Zeitschrift Universitas. Beitrag Schweitzers: "Tagebuch in Kriege." 1946.

WU—Zwischen Wasser und Urwald. By permission of C. H. Beck Verlag, München.

1—Par	21—LD	41— "
2—Kph. I	22— "	42— "
3—LD	23—Lb	43— "
4— "	24—LD	44— "
5— "	25— "	45— "
6—Par	26—KJ	46— "
7—KE	27—LD	47— "
8—Par	28— "	48— "
9—LD	29— "	49— "
10—Ex	30— "	50— "
11—Str. A	31— "	51— "
12—KE	32— "	52— "
13— "	33— "	53— "
14—LD	34— "	54— "
15—Afr. G	35— "	55— "
16— "	36— "	56— "
17— "	37— "	57— "
18— "	38— "	58— "
19—WU	39— "	59— "
20—LD	40— "	60— "

61– "
62– "
63–WU
64–LD
65– "
66– "
67– "
68– "
69– "
70– "
71– "
72– "
73–Tgb
74– "
75– "
76– "
77– "
78– "
79– "
80– "
81– "
82–LD
83–CW
84– "
85– "
86–LD
87–KE
88– "
89–Ind
90–LD
91– "
92–Jb
93–Goe
94– "
95– "
96–B
97– "
98– "
99– "
100– "
101–LD
102–B
103– "
104– "
105– "
106– "
107– "
108– "
109– "
110– "
111– "
112– "
113– "
114–H-Kn
115–SRVbl
116–SThU
117– "
118–LD
119–LJ
120–MP
121–LJ
122–Mess
123–LJ
124– "
125–LD
126– "
127–KE
128–LD
129– "
130– "
131– "
132– "
133– "
134– "
135– "
136–Kph. I
137– "
138– "
139– "
140– "
141–Oslo
142–LD
143–KE
144– "

Acknowledgments

Acknowledgment is gratefully made to the following publishers for permission to reprint and translate from the works of Albert Schweitzer: George Allen & Unwin Ltd., London; Beacon Press, Boston; C. H. Beck Verlag, München; A. & C. Black Ltd., London; Breitkopf & Härtel Verlag, Wiesbaden; Dodd, Mead & Company, New York; Harper & Brothers, New York; Freies Deutsches Hochstift Frankfurter Goethe Museum, Frankfurt; Holt, Rinehart and Winston, New York; Kommissionsverlag der Strassburger Druckerei und Verlagsanstalt; the Macmillan Company, New York; Richard Meiner Verlag, Hamburg; J. B. C. Mohr Verlag, Tübingen; Verlag Philipp Reclam, Stuttgart; and Mr. G. Woytt, Strasbourg.

The English-language publishers who gave permission for new translations of works to which they held translation rights are named under the proper titles in the list of references.